WINGSPAN

Spread your WINGS.

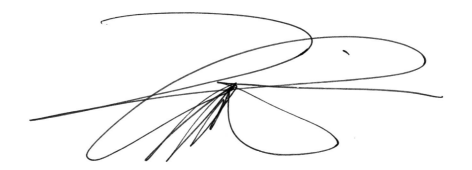

Wingspan

poems by

Kai Coggin

Golden Dragonfly Press
2016

Praise for WINGSPAN

Kai Coggin's first collection, *Periscope Heart*, was the spectacular debut of a poetic voice that the world needed to hear, a classically educated, peculiarly modern scholar with a cosmopolitan outlook and an irresistible southern charisma; it was a book that her editor described as 'the sound of wings opening.'

Her second book, *Wingspan*, takes the next logical step and launches her into brilliant and beautiful flight. She dips and soars through sensual and poignant autobiography; she tackles relevant, current societal problems like a raptor tearing into racism, body shaming, and gender identity oppression. Again, she demonstrates her agility, grasping classic images like the lips of a lover or the emptiness of grief on one page, then scooping up themes like #blacklivesmatters by their hashtags. She blends currency and radical activism with a steady, timeless devotion to the art and beauty of lyric poetry.

It's hard to follow a truly successful debut; it was a feat too difficult for Harper Lee, Robert Pirsig, or Emily Bronte. *Wingspan* not only lives up to the high expectations set by Kai's first collection; it surpasses them on every level. If you're a returning fan, you won't be disappointed. And if this is your first time meeting Kai Coggin, I have good news for you— you're about to take a flight you'll never forget.

—Del Greer, Author of *Forgotten Phone Numbers*

Wingspan is broad enough, compassionate enough, to summon and shelter readers who are often left outside the margins of the literary realm. In poems which challenge us to live with greater openness and courage, Coggin addresses the natural world, the spirit, and women's embodiment. She offers several lush poems addressed to a lover and, in part, to the reader as well: "I have spent decadent lifetimes waiting to be yours, / waiting to be in line to the throne of your mouth." This is a book built for usefulness and delight.

—Diane Seuss, Author of *Four-Legged Girl*

Kai's voice transcends earth and travels into the universe while pulling readers inward, toward their inner selves. Her words are bright, warm, and sensual. Her poems are invitations to seek your best self from within—not necessarily an easy stroll, but a journey all the same.

—Trish Hopkinson, Author of *Pieced into Treetops*
http://trishhopkinson.com

Kai Coggin has opened her wings wide with *Wingspan*. Join Coggin on this journey of poetry that has her not only opening her wings and inviting the world in, but also peeling away every layer she's accumulated down to the marrow. Her second full-length collection of poetry fights and flies with light and language that is needed to face the harshness of life. It is a catalogue of love, pain, activism, spirit, desire, beauty, evolution, and with pieces like *Presidential Tears, Black Boy Down* and *Changing My Own Name*, it is unabashed truth—the type of brutal truth that the world requires to move forward. This book seals her place as one of the most important QPOC voices in poetry today. With *Wingspan*, Kai has grown and morphed into a poetry powerhouse.

—Sarah Frances Moran, Founder & Editor of *Yellow Chair Review*

American author Kurt Vonnegut wrote, "The arts are not a way to make a living. They are a very human way of making life more bearable. Practicing an art is a way to make your soul grow, for heaven's sake. Do it as well as you possibly can. You will get an enormous reward. You will have created something." Kai has done just that. We put ourselves out there, we risk ourselves with our art, and we in turn seek out the artists who do so. As Kai writes, "This is how we recognise each other, when we are looking with the eyes of our Souls."

—Braja Sorensen, Author of *Yoga in the Gita | Lost & Found in India*

Wingspan is a book about becoming, transforming, and unfurling into the fullness of selfhood in all its disparate parts. "Hug yourself," the poet invites us, to "pull in all the skin and flesh/ so that a mountain forms/ across your chest/ from which a sun can rise," in celebration of a totality that is hard-earned and triumphant. In her sensual, full-hearted lyrical verse, Kai Coggin takes us on a journey of self-creation, self-acceptance, and self-actualization in an exploration of her multiple identities: daughter, woman, woman of color, woman of mixed race, woman who loves women, and woman of words. In the erotic feminist tradition of Sharon Olds and Adrienne Rich, Coggin locates these acts of naming and creation within the female body in a collection that swoops, soars, and delves deeply into the complexities of race, gender, sexuality, nationality, and family.

—Wendy Chin-Tanner, Author of *Turn*

CONTENTS

⌘ *Fight* ⌘

⌘ *Flight* ⌘

ACKNOWLEDGEMENTS

I would like to thankfully acknowledge the following publications in which versions of these poems have previously appeared.

Third Person — *ANIMA* & *Blue Heron Review*

Night Swimming — *ITWOW: In The Words of Womyn Anthology 2015*

Falling in Love with My Body — *Lavender Review* & *Women's Spiritual Poetry*

Into Stillness — *Harbinger Asylum*

Everything Silver / Artemis and Her Lover — *Eternal Haunted Summer*

With This Kiss — *Harbinger Asylum*

Dry-spell Ocean — *Snapdragon*

For the Majestic, One Year After The Fire — *The Sentinel Record*

Planting An Acorn After A Massacre — *Elephant Journal* & *La Bloga*

Washed-Up Dinosaurs — *La Bloga Floricanto for Fukushima Tribute 2016*

Blood-forgetting — *BROAD!*

Black Boy Down — *SunStruck Magazine*

Muddy Waters — *Split This Rock*

Standing Where A King Once Stood — *The Sentinel Record*

Every Black Boy is a Lion — *Yellow Chair Review*
(Pushcart Prize Nomination)

Presidential Tears — *Drunk Monkeys (Writer of the Month)*

I forgot my name — *Where Journeys Meet: The Voice of Women's Poetry*

How to Make a New Year's Resolution — *Yellow Chair Review*

This Body — *ITWOW: In The Words of Womyn Anthology 2016*

There Will Be An Orchard / I Throw Fruit into the Gully — *Drunk Monkeys*

An Open Letter to My Arm Flaps — *Drunk Monkeys (Writer of the Month)*

Changing My Own Name / Kai & Kimberly — *Some Talk of You & Me*

Twilight, A Study — *Ouachita High Country*

Mona Lisa, A Study — *Drunk Monkeys (Writer of the Month)*

Dad & The Dalai Lama — *Elephant Journal*

Becoming Vapor and Rain — *Yellow Chair Review & Women's Spiritual Poetry*

You Become Me Become You — *Women's Spiritual Poetry*

Meteor Shower/ Meeting-Her Shower — *Drunk Monkeys (Writer of the Month)*

The Chakras of God / Planetary Alignment — *The Tattooed Buddha*

The Journey to the Self — *Monthly Meditation International*

Infinite thanks and wing flutters to my family and friends who have made the manifestation of *Wingspan* possible through creative support, financial support, emotional support, guidance, giving me time and space alone to write, reading poems, hearing poems, coming to open mics, coming to my workshops, telling me to keep going, and telling me to spread my wings open for all the world to see. There are so many of you to list, but you know who you are, and I love you immensely.

Extra special gratitude to my creative sponsors Ester Coggin (mom, I love you!), Diana Rivera (sis, I love you!), Eloise Cottrell, Roxi Wallace, Greg Bates, and Heather Clenney. Thank you for believing that my words could fly. We did it!

Thank you to Jessica Bickley, who read this book before it was even a book, and helped me focus my vision and flight trajectory. Your sound advice and eagle eyes in copy editing helped me so much, but it is your friendship that makes me soar above the clouds.

Thank you to my incredible reviewers who took the time to open their hearts to *Wingspan*, and write the extra wind gusts of words it needed to get it off the ground. Diane Seuss, you are a masterpiece. Wendy Chin-Tanner, I knew that you would understand my experiences and internalize them with the care of a loving poet and a beautiful mother. Braja Sorensen, it takes an artist to know one—I see you. Trish Hopkinson, you have always been a graceful helping hand for me and hundreds of poets out there trying to bring their words to the surface. Del Greer, I can't thank you enough for the support and love you have given me from day one. I absolutely treasure you. Sarah Frances Moran, look how far we have come and how far we will continue to go together as poetry sisters. You challenge me every day.

Thank you to my amazing publisher Alice Maldonado at Golden Dragonfly Press for the meticulous care and love you put into shaping this little birdie into a beautiful, tangible thing. I so appreciate the warm partnership we shared in this process. You are a pinnacle of creative collaboration.

Immeasurable thanks to Joann Alesch Saraydarian for painting and designing a cover that could really capture my vision of *Wingspan*. It's exactly how I saw it in my mind, and you made it come to life. You paint my heart in so many colors. Gratitude for the infinite gifts that you bestow upon me with your friendship and love. You will always be the "you" my love poems sing to. I love you, Genghis, and Layla so much. You three are the poem my heart keeps writing.

Finally, THANK YOU, Dear Reader. Yes, YOU. I have so much love and appreciation for you, so much peace knowing that I can open my wings in your careful hands. This is my *Wingspan*, a deeper look at me, at the world around us, at the light we all hope to become. I hope it touches you in some way. I hope you know you can fly.

For J, M, D, G & L

I love you with my whole heart.

⌘

Fight

To be nobody but yourself in a world which is doing its best, night and day, to make you everybody else means to fight the hardest battle which any human being can fight; and never stop fighting.

E. E. CUMMINGS

⌘ THIRD PERSON

I was born cut out of the abdomen of a star,
dropped from the Heavens into chaos and form,
sky stitched up with lace to lay me down into this body,
undercurrent of becoming fire,
growing up into beacon,
filling out the empty skin of a torch.

I climb the stacked rungs of my spine,
porcelain teacup tower,
hand over hand ladder to firmament,
footsteps to light,
testament to breaking free,
I stand outside my skin,
hover over head, a halo of watching,
a ring of empathy circling around my body
waiting for the human soul to step out of the broken and sing,
to pick off the pieces of tattered promises and turn them into wings.

Do you know the silent science of disrobing,
detaching from what has built you from ground?
The moment you unrecognize mirrors,
it begins,
third person self,
omni-unpresent still, but pulling,
pulling up by golden thread,
lifting up out of body into open eyes,
into the cusp of blooming nebulae,
into stardust and atoms,
into that which doesn't shatter
in the infinite frequencies of knowing,
the vibrations of breakage and becoming whole,
this glowing eternal Self from which you fall
all way down to earth, to rise.

⌘ A Fleet of Paper Cranes

I folded a battalion,
a fleet of origami peace cranes,
their wings creased into
Japanese paper,
crisp lines,
astute beaks,
sky-pointed mouths,
peace,
with every fold,
I visualized peace,
these flat lifeless squares
becoming dimensional birds,
a murmuration of paper
ready to take flight into the world.

My hands grew familiar
with the movements after the first
two or three cranes took shape,
then it became just a physical twisting
and folding and sculpting and bending
that I did not have to really
give much attention,
just involuntary finger movement crane making,
while my mind drifted into
the broken,
the wartorn,
the unloved,
the helpless,
and I folded, and I folded,
a meditation in paper.

For days, I folded
these wingéd things,
gave them life through lines,
purpose through form,
energy focused into the most shapeless thing,
all of a sudden
in flight.

⌘ NIGHT SWIMMING (*for Aimee*)

One summer night, I was coaxed
into a spring-fed pond by a naked mermaid,
well, she was a mermaid in a past life,
but there is no mistaking a mermaid's power,
her siren song of urging,
her bobbing breasts floating candlelit moons,
her laughing and persuasion
echoing off the pine trees
and bouncing off stars…

and I might have had just enough to drink,
heard the "why the hell not?" chorus
coursing through me like a convincing diatribe,
an offering of courage to my shy and awkward body,
a chance to cross over the boundary
of what I would never do
in my right mind,
no, never skinny dip,
in the naked-night-moonlight
clothed only in the skin of a body I don't love enough,
and the night's whispers pushing me to jump.
Night swimming.

I was too afraid,
defiantly hell-noed her wishes,
shook my head to the stars,
negated the moonshine,
told the waving pine boughs to
put their hands down,
and told my friend, who walked to the water with me,
that he should jump in with her;
he just smiled as if he knew
this moment was meant for me.

The mermaid continued her chanting,
begged me to just get in,

come on, the water's fine,
and she reminded me of my kind heart,
I wouldn't just let her swim alone, would I?
Alone, in the murky unknown
of what night does to water
and wild things.
I felt a change inside me,
like she found the right key and
all of a sudden I opened up to the idea of
not-so-skinny-dipping my thick body into the
uncharted waters of spontaneity.
I had to do it!
I wanted to do it!
Just let go!
Come on, Kai!
When a moment like this comes by,
you can either remember it for being amazing,
or remember being too self-conscious, too scared…again.

In a moment of flight,
I stripped off my clothes and dropped them
to the sand and rocks and grasses that held my bare footsteps,
I boldly tiptoed to the water's edge,
and without a moment's hesitation,
I plunged into the glistening dark abyss of the moment!
The water surrounded me in a cool blanket of loving myself.
The exhilaration of night swimming
and my skin, only my skin.
I hugged the mermaid and we sank under
the cool spring water, bubbling up laughter.
Glorious splashing.
We freestyle raced across the pond,
tangled with fish that swam through our thighs and tickled our toes,
we climbed out and scooted bare butt
across a fallen tree that had made a bridge over the water,
our laughter howling, reverberating off limestone,

CANNONBALL!!!

One summer night,
I threw my clothes to the ground,
and danced a liberation dance with my naked and vulnerable body,
exposed to the night,
to the moon,
to the stars,
to the pines,
to the Mermaid,
to the Knight,
(who averted his eyes to my body as he cheered on my spirit)...

I held up the exposed body of me to the moonlight,
the body that held all the years of not being comfortable in my skin,
and, in a made memory, released my demons to the wind,
to dance naked, and renewed, and liberated from within.

⌘ A Poet's Inclination

I open my heart up so much
it sometimes takes in whole galaxies,
I swallowed three moons before it was noon
inside me they are orbiting a new sun,
there are no secrets,
nothing is too much for words,
there is a poem in this moment,
I can feel it, can't you?

There is not a mountaintop that does not hold my name,
I am covered in sand, scratched into earth.
There is not a sky I have not breathed
and gathered in and pushed away
and flown into with colors gripped in my teeth,
this expanse lives inside
yet I am easily lost in my own circles.
There is not a sound
that I have not rocked against my naked chest,
told that it was mine to hold
until death becomes life again,
told that I would give it another sound to marry
under my tongue and they would dance and dance.
Sounds are a world of their own, you know?

I want to love every woman I meet,
tell her she is the muse who frequents my dreams,
and it is her face that makes me believe
there is such a thing as sunrise,
but I just put all of that wanting into these poems,
these countless lines that define existence from my point of sky,
through the eye of a beholder that beholds her with rhymes,
I write these hyperboles,
pour out these lines into an abyss of white
and give them my last name,

marry me,

it is natural to want permanence
when everything changes,

when there is nothing to pin down
except the hopes that there will be no more pins.
I have broken every mold
I have thought to put myself in,
hand, cage, border, page.

Everyday, I am born again.
Today, I am an infant and tomorrow still.
If my hands become sponges, I can soak it all in
and remember to forget it all when I go to sleep,
remember to pronounce every star's light
before counting all the sheep,
let me have it,
let me take this to the apex of someone's burning question,
become water for me, world,
fill me with the absence of you becoming desert,
make me an ocean of your movement
and I will become the tide at dusk and the tide at dawn,
there is never too much rising, I say.

There is never too much rising.

⌘ Falling in Love with My Body

I am falling in love with my hands, matching friends,
how they touch every part of me that the night does not reach,
how they build, and hold, and break, and write,
how they soothe, and stir, and intertwine like vines of the most exotic wine,
how every time I have turned them into fists thrown through windows
    and doors,
they have returned to me, open and forgiving,
the ends of wings.

I am falling in love with my eyes,
dark chocolate orbs that meet the sky and shine,
how they can see through masks, right to the heart of a person,
how they are the beginning of every poem, discerning tools of
    observation,
how they see the micro in the macro, how they make beauty grow,
how they drink in the dance of life,
how they inspect, understand, grasp, discover,
how the eyes are not only the beholders of lovers,
windows into my spirit, with white silk curtains all the way open,
how they see, what they see, who they see
with the vision of Soul recognizing Soul.

I am falling in love with my breasts,
how they stand like humble mountains on a terrain of many hills,
how they ache and swell with the pulsing of want,
how they long to nourish a life born from this body,
how they fall, how they rise, how they softly spill into position,
mammary, glands of mamma,
how they will glow like full moons, clear beams only waxing light.

I am falling in love with my feet,
for every step they have tread in this life
and the lives that led me here,
the journey of the Soul that started with one meek step
into the valley of shadows, one more step,
and another, through and through and through,

8

how the valleys have become this illuminating summit
under the soles of two persistent travelers.

I am falling in love with my thighs,
thick creatures that rub against each other for warmth,
thunderous guards standing at the door of my lighted temple,
body hungry trees that offer skin-pillow heat,
how they are not defeated in their grand design, but aligned with
planets that have yet to be seen with the naked eye.

I am falling in love with my skin,
olive-brown stretch-marked
highways of decadence and loss,
of opening and close,
come close, closer,
and see how you make my colors rise,
how I can quickly become a reddened dawn
ascending over the horizon of you...

falling in love with me.

⌘ WRINKLES

Wrinkles
are starting to form
between my brows,
creases from squinting,
too much shine,
lines of laughter
spelling out time,
a fault line of worry
stretches the length
of my temples,
a crow dances
sometimes
by my eyes,
and I don't know
if you'd call these dimples,
but they show up when I smile,
and there are moon folds
that rock on their
crescent backs
holding up the world
under my gaze.

I could
look in the mirror
and see
the beginning
of wrinkles,
or
I could see
the universe
writing a poem
on my face
for all
the world
to see.

⌘ Voyage

People don't go on voyages anymore,
the word quest has no meaning, except on late night TV,
my last crusade was to the grocery store
and I did not go hungry,
I did not need the stars to guide me back home.

The sea doesn't call people into journey,
the only sirens we hear come with blue and red flashing,
and I need a reason to break out of this social obedience,
something to give my name to, an odyssey to begin,
I know heroes who have no battles to fight,
their swords, rusted metal,
their breastplates lackluster sheen,
the daylight fading from their eyes as they search
every horizon that forgets their names in a procession of apathy.

In my mind, I am a ship.
The word VOYAGE is painted across my starboard side,
the word GHOST is painted on my port side,
VOYAGE faces the dock where the heroes enter one by one,
dragging their weapons and glory behind them.

I have drunk the volume of the sea,
my lungs buoyed in my gut,
internal waves and saltwater smile,
I will push off this frenzied shore, filled with
the hope of ages reincarnated and waiting for some distant victory.

We sail in circles, waiting for a sign.

⌘ Into Stillness

Alone, I paddle out to where blue becomes deeper
and reflective tints of sunlight dance among waves,
where splashing drops of ocean nourish
the glimmering gold of my bare skin.
Oar in hands, weapon of wave gliding,
riding high upon the strength of solitary Self under sun and sky,
there floating, finally, the internal symphony of "I,"
the realization of the golden strand which resonates through my being,
once blocked from both ends,
Hell and Heaven,
now free in the sea,
on the flotation device of my Soul,
the anchor of my unfolding spirit,
necessary in its heaviness and gravity at one time,
now reflecting upward as an arrow in the sky,
propelling my beauty to the stars that I call home.

Alone, I grip tightly my rod of winged freedom and caress
each crest of wave and wind that guides me,
single traveler on unbroken horizon of ocean, stride by glorious stride,
until the silence of ONENESS stops me
and I am frozen in communion with the Universe.
I lay, naked soul, across the bough of bobbing kayak,
my transformed body, a sacrifice to the ocean above and the ocean below,
a purging of all that does not serve the striving of my heart,
the ever-pulling force of my oars to soar,
to transform into the wings of a Phoenix rising from fire and water into flight,
from darkness of unknown to realization of Light.
I fly into waves and crash through into stillness, into the calmness of
    cosmos within,
cosmos eternal and infinity in every drop of ocean and glimmer of light
    prismatic circling me.
Alone.
All One.
I am one with reflections, with light dancing, with sunset, with waves,
    with wind,
with the stillness of God inside me.

Alone, on solitary boat, floating high,
Figi fire in my eyes, erupting through my fingers,
pulsating through thick arms and thighs,
pushing and pulling God and sky and sea,
to finally reveal the stillness and beauty of Me.

⌘ THE EDGE OF THE WORLD

The ocean keeps coming,
keeps pressing its weight in waves to the waiting lip of the shore
and falling back on its own shoulders,
wave after wave,
wave after wave,
coming to kiss me,
bowling me over with its consistency of movement,
pulling me in as I stand still.

It's much easier to see the edge of the world from here,
vantage point that overlooks
cusps and fringes,
limits and periphery,
standing on the shore at sunrise looking out across the morning roar of
    the sea,
the horizon lays on her back and says *conquer me.*

Conquistadora,
I begin swimming in my mind,
stroke after stroke over pounding wave,
make my body an ancient ship,
my arms the tallest sails catching the winds in my fingers,
circumnavigate the failed voyages,
the bones of boats and men that lie
beneath the surface of this moving ocean,
I am steadfast,
part Siren, part Odysseus,
part song, part sword,
there is a map in my bloodstream,
a compass tucked behind my sternum,
my feet tingle in the sand of the shore,
in my mind the edge of the world
                            is just over the next wave,
the planetary waterfall that ends all,
the point from whence
I will jump off and...
                become

                the

                sun.

⌘ Everything Silver / Artemis and Her Lover

From the attic of my heart,
I witness his prostration to the filling moon,
the lunacy of his wanting,
the swerve of his neck to reach his white flick of tail.
I watch him preen his ripe and tufted fur,
willing centaur,
half deer, once an unbroken man,
antlers forming,
piercing through skin to touch the night with longing,
constellation branched points of bone
that call Artemis down from moon-filled sky.

Artemis,
huntress with bow,
arrow of lust,
moon rumor of requited love that wakes his body from its hooves,
evaporating desire in carnal spray on trees,
she sees him, hunted,
her silver eyes recognize the prey of her last full moon,
now bloomed into this man-beast,
with his agile limbs and quick feet,
he bucks and grazes on wild berries,
staining his lips with the blued hue of night,
to welcome in the paleness of her milky way bosom.

There is a scar on his right shoulder blade,
from where her arrow pierced his flesh.
He broke off the shaft,
did not pull the arrow through
so as to have a part of her inside him always
I watch their love-making,
a beautiful dance of limbs and weaponry and silver,
everything silver,
the pale Artemis and her man-deer, her dear man.
When the tidal currents of ocean swell
again to meet the night,

I will watch them,
the hunter and the hunted,
these lovers mounted in the stars,
I will watch them,
and wish for an arrow to fall from the sky into my open heart.

⌘ How?

How would you do it?
How would you tell me
this was love if it were?
If it is, *love*.
What colors are you made up of today?
Whose faces do I mix together to form you?
Hers and hers and maybe his cheekbones,
for this is a constant fluid,
making, *love*,
this feeling of kneading the molds,
forming the clay in shapes
that shape the body of my devotion,
how?

How would you do it?
How would you approach me
and let me know that you are you,
and this is not another meandering of words
that form another unrequited love poem?
I am here,
waiting like an autumnal changing tree,
holding ten thousand red flags
just so you will see me *falling* for you,
slowly becoming naked limbs
begging not to face the cold without your warm heart,
how?

How would you do it?
How would you let me know
to stop looking, to stop searching
for your brilliant mouth among the sounds
that keep telling me I am alone with my words?
I am all ears,
and all eyes,
and every other part of me that can be opened,
arms,

heart,
hands,
heart,
let me know and I will crumble my walls to ash,
give me a sign and I'll spell out your name in splendor,
tell me you are here and I will stop
walking in these infinite circles, lifetime after lifetime,
trying to remember the touch of your lips,
your open hands meeting my skin,
that much grace,
give me that much grace,
how?

How can I keep writing these poems
when I don't even know your jawline,
your fingers,
your shoulder blades, your chest?
Address these love letters strung together
to make words that sing to a heart I have not yet held.

How will I know?

When the circles I am walking,
and the circles you are walking,
meet in a vortex of certainty reuniting,
there will be no doubt in the world
that *everything*
has been a sign,
a signal,
a red flag
waving for the beginning of this love.

⌘ With This Kiss

With this kiss,
take my words
and find them in your mouth,
the silence is our ballad,
the stillness — our dancing,
we are of another world,
standing in our bodies without movement,
but flying as whirlwinds of stars, as the waltzing soul.

My heartbeat is a riotous chanting,
it has called you since time began,
it calls you still.

With this kiss
taste my sounds
like ripened fruit
swallowed down into your chest,
pulp ringing,
singing, the way beginnings do,
my mouth is a portal,
an arrow,
the arching bow,
pulled back into an open fire
waiting to breathe
into the cavern of your face,
replace the emptiness with all of me,
the beckoning insides
that call out to me from your heart,
I hear your song in the movement of earth,
the way in which everything harmonizes into one chord,
the reverberation that I can isolate
as the hum of your bones,
I feel you in everything and in nothing at all.

With this kiss,
become the dream that I am writing,

the canvas page blank becoming full,
the requited yearning,
the wishing star and the night as it falls softly
onto my lips, with this kiss.

⌘ Deja Vu

Deja vu, from the French "already seen"
is a strange phenomenon.
A deja vu just unfolded in front of me,
a slow motion wormhole of a moment
collapsing in on itself before my eyes, implosion.
As soon as I said to myself,
"I'm having a deja vu," it started to dematerialize,
deconstruct itself into another moment,
release its hold of illusion on time and space
and fold itself back into this seeming reality in which I
wake up and write poems into the white space of *cyberia*.

The scattered objects on my desk,
dog-eared poetry books,
a blinking light,
more poetry books,
envelopes holding letters,
uncapped pens,
a wilting orchid plant,
my eye movement on computer screen,
the cold of morning radiating off the window next to me,
frozen hands pounding out keys, joining words,
as I start another poem,
and there it was,
a deja vu,
a split second of life on repeat,
the intersection of short-term and long-term memory,
a moment that I have had before,
or a moment that I have dreamed of having.

Deja vu is a vacuum,
it is time and space trying to catch up with itself,
it is circular truth trapped in linear enforcement,
it is prophecy and permission unveiled,
it is glimpsing deeper in unraveling,

it is peering from out of body, seeing as Soul,
it is consciousness that remains nameless,
but we have all felt it, haven't we?

When a moment unfolds and shakes you from the numbness,
and you know you have been here before,

you know, for a moment, you are where you should be.

⌘ I Hold Open a Door *(inspired by V.L. Cox)* *

* *Written just months before the Supreme Court ruling on Same-Sex Marriage, when Arkansas Governor issued a pseudo-veto on HB 1228, the Religious Freedom Restoration Act*

How can you use religion
to HURT another human being?
Doesn't that go against your religion?
How can you hold your definition of God
like a gun in your hand, aiming at the faces of different?
How can a premise for faith and morality
inflict so much ugliness and suffering?

This is the history of war in the world,
the zealots and fundamentalists
that contort words into swords
and guns and missiles and drones,
and *my God* is stronger that your God,
my religion is the *real* religion.
This pathway leads to the falling of empires,
the genocides of innocents,
rampages of ages disguised as religious freedom,
well, your freedom takes away someone else's freedom,
burdens someone else's livelihood,
dampens someone else's dreams,
and if your God moves you to hate,
maybe you should think about who you are following.

Please separate your church
from my state of mind!

Please separate your church
from my state of mind!

The steps of the Arkansas state capitol
are covered in rainbow footprints,
in the temporary applause of stonewall hands,

an artist has created a series of doors
displayed on the steps that starkly remind viewers
of the separative and repressive injustices of discrimination,
some want to keep these doors closed,
to keep out the spectrum of humanity
in all of its diverse forms,
to strain out all of the colors,
but today, there are glimpses of movement
and the voice of progress is dying to be heard,
the faint chanting rally cry of equality
reaching like defiant whispers to legislative ears,
and maybe the wheels of change will
quit grinding backwards in this state
that will surely *hang* itself
with its *bible belt,*
from a beautiful old tree
in the 3 million-acre national forest
that no one will come to visit,
if we proclaim
fundamentalism over humanity,
backsliding over progress
bigotry over tolerance.
hate over love.

Please separate your church
from my state of mind.

Some businesses will close their doors,
say, "gays are not welcome here,"
say, "I won't bake a cake for your gay wedding,"
say, "God made Adam and Eve, not Adam and Steve,"
but
as for me,
I hold open a door.

I hold open a door
in my chest
in my heart,
and I just keep opening it,

I hold open a door for ALL to walk through,
have a seat,
pull up a chair,
let's talk about this struggle
and how much it has made us stronger,
but how we just don't want to have to *fight* to LOVE.

I hold open a door,
come in wrapped in a rainbow,
tell me your love story begins with,
"when I met her, she kissed all the pain away,"
tell me when you came out to your parents
they only hugged you longer
and said "I love you" until you believed it,
tell me what pronoun fits your genderqueer identity
and I will call you whatever you want
that makes you feel HOME.

I hold open a door,
you can sit down in my chest
where it is safe,
where it is quiet,
until all this noise dies down
and everyone finally sees that
people are people, are people, are people, are people.
Not one over another.

I hold open a door,
you are welcome here,
come in,
sit down,
have some coffee,
pour yourself a drink,
you are not alone,
I wrote you this poem,
I wrote us this poem.

⌘ Letter to Little Me About Loving Women

Little One,
you're beautiful,
those bangs shaping
the tiny almonds of your eyes,
did someone tell you that you could not fly?
that you could not go
where your little heart goes,
in the direction of a woman's arms?

Little one,
you will feel the *sweetest* love,
there will be a first kiss that
builds a planet of light inside you,
keep that light, okay?
Love will call you by name,
but will also deny your name
and even forget your name,
and you will feel the deepest hurt,
but you will make it through,
it is all preparation,
it is all a getting ready,
everything is just a process
of getting ready
protect your little heart during those first loves,
but feel everything,
through and through,
you are tender,
always be tender,
always stay tender
even when there is fire all around you.

It's okay, little one,
it just takes a bit of waiting,
but your bright heart will meet its twin,
she will love you,
oh, she will love you,

and teach you about beautiful things,
and take you on adventures that will become poems,
and together you will plant seeds
that you can witness turning
into wild gardens
with the patience of fearlessness,
little one, she will love you,
and become the air
that sails underneath
your tiny flapping,
she will lift you
to the heights
where your young bright light
can become a rainbow
that everyone knows by name,
don't fear the military machine
that screams at your flame...
don't fear the bigots and the zealots,
they are playing a different game,
they are people with closed eyes,
don't listen, little one,
just shine with all your heart
and their voices will get drowned out,
you will save lives just by being who you are.

I know your feet
hold tiny footsteps now,
little one,
but they will grow,
they will become mighty,
they will step into chasms that
you will turn into mountains with your bright light,
oh, tiny bright light,
do not fear,
there is always someone who knows the sound of your song,
There is always an angel who is already inside you,
who is holding a name tag that says
"Little one's soul."

You are protected,
You are guarded,
You are a holy beauty,

do not fear,
just be the flame that you have been from the start.

You are a tiny piece
of Eternal Art.

⌘ ARE YOU FLIRTING WITH ME?

If I answered your question truthfully,
"are you flirting with me?"
I would tell you how I have already turned
your bottom lip into a poem a hundred times,
shaped your chin into a place to rest my kisses
and taken your hands into my steeple,
make a prayer out of me,
turn me inside out and holy underneath your touch.

Yes, I am flirting with you.
Yes, I am trying to make you see
without seeing that I have loved you
for more days than I can remember to count.
A thousand times I think of you,
whisper your name into the quiet space,
that is the invisibility of this desire,
that is the longing that stays with me,
but is barely opening up to you,
because I have taken the time,
I have paced this wanting,
I have formed this yearning out of lust and air,
and now it is a real, breathing thing,
your body, almost the trembling ground
I can maneuver with my fingers,
your voice, that answers back and asks,
"are you flirting with me?"

So much more,
so much more than flirting,
I am flirting with danger, with uncertainty,
with a growing hope swelling in my chest,
to think that we could make a fire out of our willing bodies,
out of our vacant mouths howling for a lover
we have yet to know in each other,
my untethered heart
is moving toward the fencepost of your standing
up for something as beautiful as this.

Yes, I am flirting with you.

⌘ Reaching, and an Exquisite Jawbone

I am reaching again,
abysmal wanting,
a desire that does not
have a place to land,
a bird in my hand
with no sky to fly in,
just outstretched wings
and walking in circles,
boring holes into my desperate palms
hoping the sun will shine through.

This morning,
for one moment,
I put all my ache into
a photo of a woman's
exquisite jawbone,
her red puckered lips
created chisel of bone,
soft arching line
I could fit my words around,
exquisite, how I would kiss it,
move my mouth to the shadow
under her ear and live there,
just live there
to witness
light
becoming more light.

How just the partial view of her neck,
the lower left quadrant of her face,
could give me a home.

I am reaching again,
looking for strangers
to sing these hymns to,
these songs of wanting,

skin,
touch,
madness,
dance,
there is no ear that these words
fall into and become mountains,
that these longings become less
than longing and more than silence,
can you hear
how
my heartbeat
quivers under starlight,
hoping there is moon that we can share,
I am reaching again,
are you there?

Love?

Are you there?

⌘ PISTACHIO

i crack open / pistachio shells / one by one / listen to the dry / split whip sound / wonder when someone will / open me again / savor / what is inside / i am becoming / dry shell ash-powdered /desert waiting / for hands / to find something worth finding / in my breaking / in my splitting open / in my spilling / out toward hungry / mouth

⌘ A Room for You

I am building a room for you in my heart.
No walls, only windows.
Nothing that keeps you in,
or keeps you out.
The light will still hit your face
in these slants of touch that angle the lines
your mouth makes in waiting,
the stillness of your cloud-pulling
is welcome to stand in the quiet of your upturning chest.

I want only to touch you,
to kiss your neck,
to let you know
that my body makes a good home.
You don't have to live here,
but it is yours,
only yours,
this forever open door,
this trust I have put
on you to fill this internal aching,
this missing,
how I am missing you
yet I have never loved you,
never held the breath that welcomes
you into my world,
you are missing from me,
and I have turned all these thoughts of you
into building,
into this glorification of nothing
into everything, where you have a home
that is unknown to you,
a room that I am building inside me,
no bricks or mortar,
no wooden studs,
no nails,
just this flesh,
just this softness,
this roomful of windows
that lets the light in and waits.

⌘ Transubstantiation

I will write you into life,
I would write the word mouth
on every surface
of my skin,
mouth,
just to write you into kissing,
into breathing,
into speaking the familiarity
of my name against your lips,
you are of the air,
a figment in a creative imagination
that sends shooting stars up my spine,
circles planets with new rings,
I have not met you
but I know you are there,
I have not felt you
but I feel you always, here,
this reason to go on,
to keep writing these love poems
on the lines of invisible ethers,
on the cosmic dust that settles
on my eyelids
another night
that I lie awake
writing you into being
with my thoughts,
with my words,
eyes,
nose,
chin,
cheekbone,
jawline,
mouth again,
because I love it so,
I will write these words

in the shape of your face,
find the home
I know
belongs to me.

I will write you into life,
the shape of your hands,
hungry, open things,
waiting
to be filled
with my willing heart,
your wrists,
arms,
chest,
back,
just words now,
not skin,
I write,
I write,
I wait for something
to make this holy enough to be,
transubstantiation of intangible words
that become flesh and love
and blood and body.

I will write you into life.

mouth,
eyes,
heart,
eyes,
heart...

⌘ GIFT

My untethered heart
is gathered in a pool at your feet,
magnetism pulls me to your bones,
I want to build a house
out of the stacks of your calcified rock and marrow,
live under the roof
of your mouth,
where the rain can't touch me
but I can touch the rain,
the rain of your sound moving through me
in a prism of colors,
the way you shape poems out of heartbreak,
and bend back my yearning time and time again,
I am aching to remake the future you won't give a chance,
this is just a beginning that has already ended,
and I just want to be the someone you call out to,
the quiver in the voice box of your desire,
I'm holding a fire
for you,
lighting up another night
so you can see me in the dark,
in this space between reality and dream,
where I am a flagpole and you are the wind,
blow through everything that I am holding, love,
and make me your banner, the symbol of your coming.

I don't know what your arms feel like when they are not rushed,
when I don't have to kiss your neck in a fleeting
wisp of bravery, the open space under your right ear,
where I planted a waiting seed
that whispers love poems to you while you sleep.

You talk about love like it is all you ever wanted,
like the mirror has forgiven you,
and you're ready to stop bleeding on everything you touch,
but you can't be an open window

and a closed door.
Tell me where the lock is so that I can become a key.
Tell me where you keep the welcome mat
so I can walk through the doorframe of your shoulders.
Tell me how to turn this pain into a window.
Tell me how to quiet this eternal sounding of your name in my head,
a battle cry in the war waging against my loneliness,
a birdsong in a forest without trees,
the fallen leaves building a blanket that can't keep me warm,
the stars that see the sun, and become fading prayers.

You are hiding your lips behind a flower,
and I will name
every petal "she loves me"
until I reach your kiss.

My untethered heart,
I've shaped it into a gift
that I keep leaving at your door,
and you keep staring out your open window,
waiting for someone to love you.

⌘ Balcony

I woke up with you
on my lips again,
this name,
this face,
this mouth
that I feel in my heart is mine,
    yours,
you have been a repeated dream,
over and over
a welcome in the night
to open my heart again and let you in,
though, when we are both awake,
living our completely separate lives,
there is no mention of this,
no yearning from your end to mine,
no longing to find the other half of you
in the distant possibility of me.

I would throw the tiniest pebbles
at the closed windows of your eyes
to wake you from this solitary life and
sweep you back into our soul agreement of dreams
where we are learning to love each other again
on some level we can not yet feel, but
I am down here waiting
holding a bouquet of time I want to give you,
and I would Romeo the wildest tree
to find the balcony of your bottom lip,
the lip that I have contemplated for lifetimes,
how I would start there,
slowly,
how I would only start where your words finish
and maybe you would leave
a poem in my mouth
or we could write one together,
how our tongues could form a new language
we are both waiting to hear
through the silence between us.

⌘ A Shipwreck

"light seals the cracks"—Rita Dove, *Grace Notes*

I am still
finding cracks,
holes where your
hands once were,
I am taking on water,
looking for something to fill me
something to fulfill me,
full fill filling feel feeling,

I undergo
what looks like love
to prevent what looks like loss,
and I sweep up
the broken shards
that slip sometimes from my mouth,
and you are still the glue,
the binding together
of my shattering,
you are still my starboard glory
teaching my throat to dance,
teaching my hands to unwaver,
stay the course,
lead our bodies to the shore
we know only as love,
we traced the island expanding
beneath our feet, in the ancient maps
we found in each others chests,
treasure,
your true north heart,
Magellan mouth,
circumnavigate my globes with your lips,
equator my hips with your hands,
follow only the stars in my eyes,
they will take you home,

and when my bodies fracture
into an evolution of upward opening,
I will look at myself through your eyes
and see the light pouring forth
from inside my holy wreckage.

⌘ Dry-spell Ocean

I have been
sitting
at the edge of
my own mouth,
chewing on
my own silence,
perched on the boulder
of my chin
waiting for an aurora
of words
to finally blanket my horizon
with something other than drought,
with something other than
fog grey doubt and comparative hesitation,
this space has been absent,
a void of echoes,
a quarry of whispers that tell me
to put my pen down,
my voice buried in sand,
mouth agape
digging for the sake of depth,
in this unintentional hush.

I have been
sitting
at the edge of
my own mouth,
skipping flat wet stones across my tongue,
beating heart sounds with a stick
against my hollow teeth,
knowing that this is a river,
that this is a stream
of consciousness
that will always lead me to a place
I thought I had lost,
a place I think I will lose again,

that temporary space where I
know myself as poet/writer/artist/muse,
without confusing me with
everything I refused to be in the lifetimes
before when abuse was me.

This pacing of sounds,
this holy unfurling of verse
rises up like a blaring sun
from the gorge of my windpipe,
I can feel the breeze now,
the heat,
I can feel a breath of clarity/poetry,
a calm steady wind
blowing me upwards,
the sun of my own voice
painting everything golden.

My mouth,
my own mouth
not a river,
but the moving ocean.

⌘ From the Edge of a Willow Tree

I once met a willow tree on the shoulder of a shore
who doesn't remember the sound of wind,
only knows the way water feels
on her fingertips, has become just that wetness,
become that level of constant movement in waves,
her branches and limbs and heavy swaying trunk
are left to wonder about purpose,
about why one feeling can be more powerful than another,
about how wind has ultimately lost to water
and there is more emptiness
than drinking in.

I remember what the sky looks like when I close my eyes,
the sun has burned a white hole into my heart,
and I can let it go if I want to,
or I can fly into it
until tomorrow is no longer something I wait for,
but something that waits for me.

I know there is power in these hands,
the tips of my fingers hold unwritten gospels,
and each word can become someone's blessing,
someone's rope to sinking ship,
someone's hand outstretched that looks like a savior
but is only

a poem.

There is saving to be done here, but all that is holy is the
opening of hearts, the opening of mouths about to shout poems
to the dark of another emptying night,
the tipping point between pain and release
that can bring the sunlight back into the horizon of an aching chest.

I am here to fall in love.
I am here to light a candle that I have held forever.
I am here to name the spark-voice inside me every name that is *beautiful*.

Hold me up against the light,
and see the crimson glow shine through my skin,
I want to be red and alive, I want to be read with the world's eyes.
Do these words float?
Do they hold water or return to the sea?
Is this a life raft I am paddling around,
or would I make more ripples sitting completely still,
just listening to the morning become an unwritten song of colors?

I like the feel of water on my fingers,
my hands becoming waves,
my eyes like distant stars that dot the night with meaning
and give the sky a new name.

⌘ For the Majestic, One Year After The Fire *

* *The Majestic Hotel is a famous historic hotel in Hot Springs National Park, Arkansas. It burned to the ground on February 27th, 2014.*

Majestic (adjective): having or showing impressive beauty or dignity

There's a hole in the sky
where the Majestic once stood,
now just bricks, bent steel,
broken windows and wood.

If you squint your eyes,
you can still see her structure shadowing
in the setting sun against the pines,
a silhouetted madam that
became a temporary home
for travelers bathing in the
healing Hot Springs waters,
for baseball players
who wore Red Sox and
hiked West Mountain for training,
for Mafia crime lords
who found a peaceful respite
and called a truce in the lobby of her mahogany belly.

There's a hole in the sky
where the Majestic once stood,
now just bricks, bent steel,
broken windows and wood.

I walked around the rubble
on a warm February day,
almost a year after the building
caught fire and became a memory of ash.
I wanted to see what she had become,
wallow inside her leftover bones
stand in the middle of her incendiary decimation,
a wasteland of remains underfoot,
vines grow up and around

the piles of asbestos bricks
a year after crumbling,
jagged contortions of steel spell out
the negligence of man,
there is a ladder that points up to the sky,
jutting out of her Majestic heart, reaching nowhere,
hoping for some kind of revitalization,
or at least for someone to pick her body up off the street,
this broken building, bleeding wreckage.

There's a hole in the sky
where the Majestic once stood,
now just bricks, bent steel,
broken windows and wood.

A fire escape still clings to the side
of the red building,
the portion of the resort that still stands,
empty and useless,
but still stands,
the fire escape an ironic display
of what did not escape fire,
this landfill of history,
the fallen walls of so much joy and decay,
I look up into a corner room,
broken window open
that overlooks the graveyard of the burned,
I think of the spirit of the building
and a ceiling fan starts turning
a slow, painful song.

There's a hole in the sky
where the Majestic once stood,
now just bricks, bent steel,
broken windows and wood.

There is beauty in the wreckage,
her lines and shadows are sharp faces of sorrow,
the cut glass of forgotten cheekbones,
she is pale and abandoned,
dusted in cinder and ash,
the inverted womb of a once bustling city,

now a pyramid of loss,
a mountain of handing-off-blame,
a broken heap of history, her-story was Majestic,
we must pick up her broken pieces,
and build a clean slate, a stronger community,
a city government that hears the song of its people,
no more vacant caves ready to burn,
we must take this loss as a lesson well learned.

There's a hole in the sky
where the Majestic once stood,
now just bricks, bent steel,
broken windows and wood.

There's a fire in my heart
for this fallen Queen,
her legacy is now a sacrifice,
a tipping point
in the saving of this beautiful town,
we must save the stories,
the magic,
the healing,
the arts,
the buildings that lined the
streets of America's first playground,
we must come together,
pick up the pieces of all the yesterdays
and build a golden tomorrow
with the unwavering bricks and mortar of community,
with the clear windows of unbreakable vision,
with the solid wood frame of cooperation,
with the steel promises of a Hot Springs Spirit,
the healing water that runs through our veins,
the valley's vapor that is our collective sigh of relief,
knowing something beautiful will come of this loss.

There's a hole in the sky
where the Majestic once stood.

If we can build something from her ashes,
we should.

⌘ Dishes & Stigmata

Last night,
while doing the dishes,
a broken glass meeting granite countertop
stabbed stigmata on my right palm,
a deep wound, open mouth spewing blood
until I was holding a pool of everything
warm and red and flowing inside,
outside,
collecting,
deep,
dark.

When you are hurt,
you want to know how severe the wound is.
I opened the cut and revealed my inner flesh,
pink squishy brains in hand,
a quarter of an inch deep,
half an inch wide, red,
as I opened it and looked inside.

Shock is a strange endorphin.
I showed her the gory sight with cucumber calm.

She poured cayenne powder
into the bleeding gorge,
cauterizing the throbbing stab,
you would think it would burn more,
fingers turning cold,
under the faucet
blood orange swirling
down drain,
she wrapped my fist like a prizefighter,
I'm glad to have her in my corner.

I thought of the scar this would become.

My father had a scar from the Korean War on his right palm,
stopped a bayonet from going through him
by grabbing the blade and looking death in the face.
I don't know what happened after that.

That scar saved his life;
his other scars were left at the bottom of a bottle.
As a child, my mother cut her pinky off with a machete,
racing against her brothers and sisters on the farm in the Philippines,
to harvest the most rice bushels,
a salve of Grandpa's wet tobacco
wrapped around the dangling digit
and a bandage from the village doctor
put the pinky almost back to its original straight stance,
but you would never notice it now
because of the two golden pinky rings that mom wears,
one on each pinky, shimmering distraction
from that crooked little finger,
I still don't know which one it is that's bent, right or left.

I look down at my bandaged hand,
the blood contained from cayenne cauterization,
just the white of gauze and tape, a cross,
just the pulling together of forced stillness and idle hands,
how the coldness of my fingers reminds me that my body
knows what it is doing, that heat is rushing to the wound,
that nature is a glorious design.

I remember the strength of my parents' hands,
individually,
collectively,
together,
apart,
far apart.

My father was a left-handed journalist,
his quick staccato typewriting done with only his index fingers,
thick and dense, holding too many secrets.

My mother's hands are secret gardens,
climbing night-blooming jasmine, butterflies,
red fingernails, forgiveness.

My right hand's sudden stigmata,
shows me my own Holy lineage,
the scar will remind me on the days I forget.

⌘ Planting an Acorn After a Massacre

When I heard the news
of the 132 school children massacred,
the taliban suicide bombers in
explosive-lined vests
blowing up the lights of brightened futures,
emptying thousands
of shell casings into the heads of innocents,
I went outside with my grief,
couldn't hold it indoors,
I walked in circles
and wondered
how the sun
could continue this charade,
how the breeze could decorate
the almost barren trees
with dancing dried skirts,
quivering leaves.
I held the hands of the sky
and whispered unknown names
into the afternoon silence,
as two turkey vultures
cut the blue by
flying infinities overhead.

I walked.
Each step accompanied
by the sound of dried leaves
crunching underfoot,
and fallen acorns shone slick
in the light of the sun,
some dusted with grains of sand
that reflected prismatically
into the tiniest rainbows,
almost invisible.
I picked one up.
It had cracked open,

its red root arm reaching out for earth,
seed sprout seeing possibility,
the process of growth
inherent in its nature.

Without question and without fail
scores of acorns around me
had split open
in these cold months,
split open and started the process of
digging themselves down into the dirt,
the brilliant design that unlocks
wooden hinges and breaks free.

I thought of the children,
their arms reaching toward futures
that they could not see
but could feel,
their brilliant design,
their chubby reddened cheeks,
their laughter,
their learning becoming
scattered schoolbooks
and bomb-blasted classrooms,

they will not become trees,

they will not get past the point
of just barely breaking through,
red blood arms shielding faces
that wonder how this could be the end,
then it is,
was,
blackness,
ending.

The innocents should not die
for a God that does not live by the moral code
that innocents should not die.
I get lost in all this,
the soft breeze,

the blood,
the peaceful valley of my home,
the massacre that touches the same earth floor
dirt on which I stand and gather bursting-open acorns,
juxtaposition of death and life,
my red root fingers dig for the meaning,
for the karmic and cosmic balance,
and all I can do is find a patch of softened moist soil,
a spot that gets good sunlight,
and I shovel a small hole with a jagged flat rock
and lay the
    acorn
    inside
    the hole
with the red root
pointing toward the planet's core.

"Something small must have a chance,"

I say to myself,
and I cover the acorn with the supple ground.

I encircle the life burial plot
with a mandala of 11 acorn caps,
(you know the little hats that acorns wear)
I make a circle,
because circles are unbroken,
because life should be unbroken,
because something small must have a chance.

I close my eyes,
and let the sun kiss me
until I am warmed inside
with the red of late afternoon,
until I see the mightiest oak tree in my mind,
132 sprawling green limbs
reaching up, up, up,
for
Heaven.

⌘ That Time

That time I was an ant,
I did not know I could carry so much.

That time I was a stone,
I valued the time that I stood still.

That time I was a bird,
I named every cloud a friend.

That time I was a shadow,
I did not know it was light that formed me.

That time I was a waterfall,
I understood what it meant to fall in love.

That time I was an ocean,
I rose to hug the moon.

That time I was a woman,
I knew the power of my womb.

That time I was a Soul,
I knew how it felt to be ALL.

⌘ WASHED-UP DINOSAURS

Sea Monsters
have been found on the shores of California beaches.
Two, in the last week.
Catalina Island, Los Angeles coast,
the first sea monster was 18 feet long,
an oar-fish, or sea serpent, that surfaced from
the dark, unknown depths of our ocean.
One of the ill-famed, mariner-eating monsters,
this lochness lookalike, this giant underwater dragon,
viking swallower, ship capsizer of ancient days,
died in such a humble and uneventful way,
washed up only 15 feet from the Catalina Island shore,
where a young marine biologist snorkeled in the afternoon sun.
She saw the flash of a silver tail shining underwater,
and dragged the half-floating sea serpent
to the sands where her friends and other beach goers
stood amazed at her catch.
Sixteen people had to carry its majestic shimmering silver
body out of the gently crashing blue water,
posing for a photo-op with this beast of Nordic lore.
Its cold silver dollar eyes and ravaged silk mouth did not smile.

There is an old Japanese legend that says
that oar-fish beach themselves as an omen to
a Great Earthquake.
A reporter said that dozens of oar-fish
were found beached days before the devastating
2011 Fukushima 7.1 earthquake in Japan.
Is this sea serpent a harbinger of impending doom?
The smiling sixteen people in the Catalina Island photo,
with the silvery banner of ocean's untimely demise
spread across their chests,
don't seem to think so.

Two days later,
another rare, great beast of the ocean

was found stranded on the shores of tourist-soaked
Venice Beach, California
of all places.
An Alaskan saber-toothed whale,
all 15-feet and 2,000 blubbery pounds of her,
washed up on shore barely alive,
surrounded by a swarm of onlookers,
some who tried to push her back into the water to save her,
and some who did nothing but took out their cell-phones
and snapped selfies for Instagram and Facebook
with the dying whale in the background,
her muted, humble whale-song the soundtrack to barbarism.

The female saber-toothed whale
does not grow the giant saber-tooth;
only the male is strapped with this magical unicorn horn
protruding down like a sword out of the side of his mouth.
The female is a calm giant,
a frigid ocean deep swimmer who prefers the waters of the Arctic
to the warm California coast.
What brings her to Venice Beach?
There was undigested plastic and spooled nylon strands in her belly.
"Not enough to cause her death," the scientists say.

Exactly how much plastic IS okay
to have permanently undigested in your belly?

Fuckers.

Washed up dinosaurs of the ocean's dark and deep womb,
stranded sea monsters, falsely-accused viking hunters,
flailing on the shallow sands of an unfamiliar coast,
Humanity's coast, where the bustling consumer landscape meets the
    water,
and destruction is the only language that nature understands.
What are these royal beasts trying to say to us that we are just not
    hearing?
I have my ear to a distant whale-song
and a sea serpent's quiet hum of liquid movement.

I have my ear to the heart of something bigger than me
that I can so easily become swallowed in...willingly.

I have my ear to a nautilus' emptied shell
    to hear the Divine Secrets of the Ocean,

            the indecipherable and infinite wishing of waves.

I am listening.

⌘ QUADRUPLE RAINBOW

A quadruple rainbow,
mother earth gives us a gift,
a sight unseen until today,
a miracle unfolded
in a prism of colors,
a double rainbow,
on a double rainbow
this is the reflection of all
the love she has for us,
this is the reflection of all
the beauty she encompasses,
her dignified chest,
her open-heart womb,
give her room to breathe
and she will write in
quadruple rainbows,
do not believe that she is not magnificent,
do not believe that we are not her tiny
(*destructive*) wonders
hoping to change
before it's too late,
before we hurt her anymore,
oh, mother
planet earth,
how you exhale in color,
how you paint the sky with hope
against the bleak background of what
we have done to you.

⌘ Escapism for my Grief (*for Emily*)

When I heard about you dying,
I put on my work boots
and a pair of thick gloves,
I went to the woodpile behind the house
took the ax in my hands,
and started splitting logs.

The heavy ax
wound back in my arms
and thrusted down onto each log
with a sound like a muted thud,
stretching fibers of wood
grasping for one another,
cracking,
splitting,
falling to pieces,
the smell of pine,
dogwood, oak.

My body was cold,
disjoined,
somewhere else,
but I just had to hit something,
had to feel this cause and effect,
this instantaneous change to nature,
this sudden breaking,
like I felt inside,
confused, stoic,
divided into the grief
orbiting your three sons,
these shattered concentric circles of wood
and how the planet of your heart
revolved around each one of those little boys.

Hours passed,
the pile of split logs was all around me, getting higher,

building a wall of wreckage that was not mine,
and I just kept standing another log on the sturdy base
and driving my sorrow into the sound of the ax,
into the halves of logs,
into the halves of lives that are left here without you making whole.
Split wood,
so much split wood,
split atoms, divided cells
a self-necessitated mitosis,
trying to bring some kind of birth to your sudden death.
I kept splitting, maybe a hundred logs,
I wanted to split the wood to paper,
three and a half hours,
I thought of you,
how you read my poems
in the few days that became the last days of life,
how my book was in the room
when your young body was released to your timeless soul,
and I hope you read the poem about dying,
the will and testament of body becoming sun,
but I know you didn't because it was at the end of the book,
and I wish I had put it near the front.

The afternoon sun fell through the trees,
a breeze slowly stripped red and yellow from branches,
creating moving autumnal fire,
creating a golden glow over this whole moment,
my hands became heavy,
I let the ax-head drop to the ground
and the handle fall over into the pile of its distant brothers.

A cluster of large maple leaves
on a thin stick coming out of the ground
glowed with green, crimson, and gold,
the ethereal light surrounding it
made me feel like you were there, Em,
and I thought of your hair,
the different hues of you in high school,
the misfit friend who fit into me

ecause sarcasm's laughter was the best kind,
and I thought of the woman you became,
the mother, the lover, the beautiful heart,
and I just let myself feel you, the maple leaves waved silently.

I built a fire that night, with all the split pieces of trees,
with the escapism I had created for my grief,
I watched it burn, turning you into light, a pyre in my heart,
saying goodbye to you, my royal friend, Emily Noel Stedorro.

⌘ Chasm

Freedom Tower,
Manhattan skyline shifting,
architectural erection of
steel and fiberglass masked with
hyper-prismatic reflections of blue sky,
changing the way we name memorial,
rising from the ashes of disaster to plaster
rebirth in 1776-foot manipulations of isosceles triangles
stacked into octagonal coronation,
sky scraping,
star grazing,
408-foot flashing spire to the night,
light emitting diode red, and white, and blue,
true to this unscathed American Spirit
shining to the rest of the world as some kind of beacon,
some kind of representation of resilience,
or at least, what it *should* look like.

This brilliant design,
the heavily-reinforced evacuation routes,
the preemptive fireproofing of the building's core,
the multiple back-ups of emergency lighting and sprinklers,
the extra-wide pressurized stairs equipped to handling
mass-hysteria and widespread panic,
just in case...
no nothing can stop that American determination
to build higher and higher and higher,
to usurp the other phallic wonders of metal and windows,
this crescendo in skyline,
this elevated pulse line on the EKG of big apple sky,
this apple of America's crying eye,
One World Trade Center,
the new tallest building in the United States of America.

Lady Liberty strains her neck to see the eager tourists
on the 104th floor observation deck, kissing clouds and

celebrating this marvel of architecture and design,
and she shudders to think of the plumes of smoke and chaos,
the falling pillars,
the war-torn scraps of buildings,
mangled steel and white rain ashes.
She keeps her silent vigil, her fiery torch aflame.
A man builds bigger and better.
A woman never forgets what was broken.

Ground Zero, where heroes were made
and more heroes were laid
to rest, free-falling to death,
burning phoenixes of lost hope and
too many tomorrows cut short,
now just names inscribed on the walls of memorial,
fingers of families tracing the letters that spell out emptiness,
father,
daughter,
mother,
son.

It doesn't matter how tall they strive to make this building,
what height records they are intent on breaking,
what history they are intent on reshaping,
how bright the beacon of light is that shines for miles around.

Heartbreak

is an empty chasm that even the tallest building in America cannot fill.

⌘ 10,000 Birds

"Comprising 88 7,000-watt xenon light bulbs positioned into 48-foot squares that echo the shape and orientation of the Twin Towers, Tribute In Light is assembled each year on a rooftop close to the World Trade Center site. The illuminated memorial reaches 4 miles into the sky and is visible from as far as 30 miles away. The two arrays cast the strongest shaft of light ever projected from earth into the night sky."

10,000 birds
into the light
twin tower
shafts of
ten thousand
who rely on
to travel to
and the night
for hunting
c i r c l i n g
falling stars
of the Tribute
ungodlyhands
into space
fly in endless
navigation of
10,000 birds
our abrasive
yes, I see the
but these are
from the same
before fatal
disregard for
in the name of

fly straight
of the fallen
m e m o r i a l
ungodly light
migratingbirds
constellations
warmer homes
sky protection
prey they glint
d i a m o n d s
this is not part
this is man's
reaching out
10,000 birds
brokencompass
these false suns
in the light of
p a t r i o t i s m
s y m b o l i s m
souls falling
windows as
light attraction
these flying lives
memorializing the

dead.

Note: NY Governor Andrew M. Cuomo just announced that state buildings will participate in the New York State Lights Out Initiative, joining the Audubon Society in the charge to reduce sources of light pollution that disrupt and disorient birds during migration. I am hoping this includes the Tribute in Light that blasts the brightest lights every year on 9/11. My thoughts go up to the millions of migrating birds.

⌘ Water Fountain Witness

I went to fill up our water jugs
at the community water fountain,
light drizzle fell creating a glistening blur
over everything, an ethereal mist.
An old man was filling his half-dozen
plastic gallon-sized milk bottles,
holding a warm smile as I approached
and started to fill my five gallon behemoth
glass jug at the next faucet.

We connected eyes, nodded our heads,
traded quick quips about the weather,
and our wishes for Spring,
his caterpillar white eyebrows danced when he talked.

"I have a gift for you," he said,
outstretching his closed-up ball of a hand.

"Oh, thank you," I accepted, reluctant and polite,
the sound of the water still gushing into my jug,
an hourglass too slow with sand.
I looked at the small token he placed in my palm,
a bright shiny penny with a thick cross stamped out of it.
"Oh, Jesus… not one of your followers…" I thought to myself.

"It cost me a whole penny."

I chuckled because he said it like a cute grandpa,
and I hoped somebody thought his little jokes were still funny.

"Jesus had to pay a WHOLE lot more.
HE had to pay with his LIFE."

He went on to tell his story,
witnessing
to his unsuspecting fellow man,

just filling up her unsuspecting water jug
on this unsuspecting drizzle of a day.

"Have you accepted Jesus as your personal Lord and Savior?"

I wanted to tell him that I was a Lesbian Jesus
in a high school dramatic skit where I
hung on a cross at a Catholic youth conference
in front of 2,000 kids,
but these days, I don't wear a bible belt,
and we find God in different ways.

I uh-huh and mmm-hmmed and when
the water splashed up onto arm,
I put the cap on my overfilling jug and said goodbye.
He was already telling a couple of young guys
he had a gift for them, and the trail of the conversation
faded as I walked to my car.

That evening,
I emptied my pockets
and found the coin, the coin with the
cross stamped out of it,
the cross punched out of copper,
a gift in negative space,
like how "Christianity" is the negative space,
and "Christ" is the actual image.

I think of the old man in Arkadelphia
who makes these cross pennies for the
witnessing old man at the water fountain,
how he must be rich with all that holy copper,
how he must be swimming in tiny crosses
leftover from all this stamping out,
the body of Christ clinking as it hits the dirty linoleum floor,
the message somewhere in all that negative space.

⌘ Blood-forgetting

Each month I bleed,
I see the absence,
as if there is something
that would have been
nourished
with my blood's thick riches,
as if a baby
could have been
warmed with the red-blanket of me,
until I could hold it close,
until I could name it

wonder
    future
light
    forever.

This body—
    warm altar,
    uterus grail,
    bloodletting forget.

I am not a battlefield—
    yet
    here is the blood that
    holds the lives of men unmade,
    women never built into towers.

Each month I bleed,
a part of me says goodbye
    to something that was never here,

    to someone that was never.

⌘ Black Boy Down (*for Michael Brown 1996–2014*)

I already wrote this poem,
Black boy down,
Officer heavy trigger finger,
I don't want to see the sun shine
through the holes you left in his body,
Black boy down,
I don't have the right to write this poem.
I got pulled over last week for a taillight out and expired tags,
never did I think I would get shot,
never did I think my life would be over,
never did I think I was public enemy number one,
never did the fear of being my own shade of light brown come into play,
I did not get frisked or patted down,
I didn't even get a ticket.
What is the difference in my life over someone else's?

I am numb from this,
Can't read anymore details,
Can't find any peace in the aftermath,
Can't find a glimmer of hope this time,
Black boy down.
Not really understanding the depths of my privilege but learning,
wanting to learn the meaning of passing through life
without carrying the fear of seeing a cop on the street who might kill me.
It's unfathomable to me, but why isn't it unfathomable for everyone?

Black boy down.
10 shots through his young black boy skin,
He was going to start college last Monday.
Literally.
His first day of school became the day the riots swelled on
the streets of Ferguson Missouri,
smoke rising from fires and looting,
the rage of a people wavering on the precipice of peaceful protest
and LET'S BURN THIS MOTHER FUCKING CITY DOWN!!

BLACK BOY DOWN!!

Black boy down
Michael Brown,
Young Mike Brown,
Brown boy,
Black boy,
Never going to be a black man,
Black son,
Black life taken before it really begun.

I already wrote this poem,
His name was Trayvon,
But I don't really own the words,
Black boy down,
This fear is not mine, but I feel it,
This rage is not mine, but it seethes in my gut,
This roaring noise rising from candlelight vigils,
Waking me from the blindness of privilege
to see a mother's blank, broken eyes
crying for her baby,
crying for her baby boy down.

Baby boy down.

⌘ Muddy Waters

"Muddy water, let stand, becomes clear"—Lao Tzu

Maybe this is still the
muddy water,
the dirt of ages,
the shame of mankind's unkindness,
the compilation of grievances
that stack like black stones,
building a wall that divides
the nation for one last time
before everything crumbles
and grows again,
grows new,
or is forever broken,
in pieces,
lost.

I cannot see through this mud,
have no answers,
only feel the wail of another black mother
cut the sky in half with her loss,
rip the thunder from the clouds with her grief,
everything taken,
broken, destroyed, gone,
another son falling over the horizon into
a night that has lasted too damn long,
this swallowed down suffering,
this racism that was designed to look like life,
that was created to pass as normal society,
the status quo of another black life
erased from history,
while justice turns another blind eye.

Muddy waters,
yes, the waters are muddled
with tears

and stomping,
and screaming,
and rage,
and dissent,
and something's got to give,
the inevitable straw has broken the camel's back,
the weight, too heavy for far too long,
the battle cries of black youth piggybacking
on the failed songs of King's and ancestors,
uprising, protesting, marching to the beat of drummers with no hands,
cries that turn to ash and fade into the dust
of another morning mourning the death of another black son.

March, brothers and sisters,
take steps toward what may seem like revolution,
but is really just another circle
around the bottom rung of a ladder that you
were always destined to hold up,
but never destined to climb.

March, brothers and sisters,
shout BLACK LIVES MATTER into the night,
though there is no real chance to sway the system
established for your annihilation,
designed for your casual degradation,
the weight of the black human soul perpetually
outweighed by the weight of white fear.

This can no longer be the reality.
This is not the reality we want for our children.
Our bones are all the same color
of stacked pieces making whole body.
Our hearts are all the same dark rich red
pumping machine of life, not death, same.
Our Spirits are all made of the same brilliant, on-going LIGHT.

March, brothers and sisters,
I hear the hum of your chanting,
I feel the tremble in the earth

of collective footsteps from New York to LA,
and move my feet with you,
pacing my living room like a caged lion,
heartbeat drumbeat banging on the walls of this invisible prison system
of thoughts and ideas and prejudices and rewritten history
and our footsteps are telling the real stories,
and our footsteps will muddy the waters,
will no longer stand for injustice,
muddy the waters,
until the blood runs clear.

⌘ Moonlight, Finding Fathers

It is moonlight,
and we walk around
the nation's capitol
with a sense of wonder,
waiting to come up slowly,
on foot,
to the glowing auras of
Great Men,
to see how they light up the night
with words like Honor, Freedom, Liberty…
how they compel the stars to shine
brighter in the sky, more with their chests out,
more with their shoulders back to lift up protruding wings,
we are *finding* Fathers.

Divine Architecture
of monumental men, pillars
that line squared off angles of angels,
masonic mausoleums of history carved into stone,
I walk alone to a corner of Lincoln's Memorial,
I read the words of "Four score.."
about the "unfinished work"
and "the proposition that all men are created equal,"
in my mind, I read the words in
what his voice
might've sounded like.
What is the intonation of unknown strength?
What noise does courage make when it is breaking the sky?
Is the color of battlefield anything but red?

It is moonlight
and I am moved by history,
I walk back to the glowing Abraham,
his lit up intentions,
his larger than life Spirit
enshrined in the Heart of a Temple,

and I look into the eyes of a stone,
and break through to the Man,
to the energy of a leader
who left a legacy that a country
could grow into.

All Men Are Created Equal.

We are still growing, Abraham.

I know that somehow,
through all of this
madness
this killing,
this shouting,
this protesting,
this #blacklivesmatter,
this, this, this aching…

we are still growing.

⌘ STANDING WHERE A KING ONCE STOOD

"The ultimate measure of a man is not where he stands in moments of comfort and convenience, but where he stands at times of challenge and controversy."
—DR. MARTIN LUTHER KING, JR.

My humble feet stand where
He once stood, A Great King.

My brown boots cast a moonlight shadow on his words

"I Have A Dream"

and a wave of surreal knocks me in the chest,
a bend in time and space,
I lift my head to the empty night in front of this glowing memorial,
and I am immediately looking out
on the sea of people that hot August day in 1963,
the sun beating on our heads
our wide open hungry hearts,
fans waving the wind in the favor of change,
and church praise *hallelujahs* rising up
for this preacher,
this reverend,
this great soil body of a man
from which an infinite garden of seeds could grow.

I stand in the exact spot where He stood,
where the sweat dripped down his legs
and beaded on his head,
reflecting stars in the daylight,
where the echoes of his words bounced back
from Lincoln's hallowed chamber,
where the grand pillars of this nation are no longer prison bars,
where his wingtip shoes might have trembled,
but the tips of his wings showed the
Power of a King
for all the world to see.

I stand.
I kneel.
I bow my head.
I kiss the ground where
a King once stood.

⌘ From His Perspective
(after the death of Freddie Gray) *

* Though I will never know the daily terror of living as a young black boy in a society built on systemic racism and the disproportionate oppression of African Americans, here my pen and my empathetic heart *try* to walk in his shoes.

I can't walk
in these shoes again,
this skin,
this eternal night,
that warrants
gunshots
bent branches
arching down limbs
that find my limbs
bent, bruised, broken,

please don't make me face
those hateful faces,
my mama ain't raise no punk,
but I'm scared, man,
I am scared,
I can turn into silence
with one quick
kill that nigg** trigger finger
to end me,
and I'm nothing, dead, gone,
jus' like that.

I can't walk
in these shoes again,
not on this night, no,
not on any night as suspect of every crime,
as public enemy number
    is up *every 28 hours*, no,
not this night,

not when I can so easily
become the darkness,
the fading out son,
the disappearing boy,
though all I hold
in my young chest is light,
is candles, is glory,
is the sound of hallelujahs
building a fortress around
my growing black boy body,
Lawd, why?
Why do my mama have to cry?
Why she have to turn on TV
to see another brother dead
floating face down
in his own pooled street blood?
Red,
it's the same color,
it's the same *damn* color
that those white cops bleed,
that we all bleed,
red,
not black,
not white,
not brown,
red,
my bones
make the sound of roses growing,
quiet whispers of a boy
becoming man.

Will I become a man?
In these shoes,
in the soles of my
always running feet,
what?
don't look at me,
don't come up on me
askin', *"boy, whatchu doing?"*

you don't know me,
where I've been,
where my mama been,
where my daddy been
how my grandpa marched with Dr. King,
actually shook that man's hand,
and here I stand
with this tempered rage and muffled joy,
the heart of a lion
in the body of a young black man.

My life matters.
MY LIFE MATTERS.

I ain't going out like that, you hear me?
My mama ain't raise no punk.
I will become a man.
I will live
and shout
and pray
and march
and laugh
and cry
and love, god damnit, I will love,
and run
until I don't have to run anymore,
until history gets the hell off my back
and I can stand
and spread
these wings
that have been
tied down
with chains
for too damn long.
I will FLY.

I WILL FLY.

My life matters.

MY LIFE MATTERS.

⌘ Upon Hearing Two White Men Sing Dixie at Open Mic, After the Charleston Massacre/ (Don't) Look Away, Dixie

Yes, I know this is the south,
this is your heritage,
your southern identity,
the flag of Arkansas
looks like a disguise
dressed in rebel red,
inverted intentions reflecting
the same colors,
the same lines,
the same meanings
when they flap boldly in the wind,
a limp cloth of hate,
it's hard to tell the difference,
there is no difference,
and I can smell a cross burning as they sing

Dixie,
that boyhood harmony
sung from the gentle poet hearts
of two kind old white men at open mic,
still echoes like an unnamed horror,
still permeates the air
with visions of slave ships and cracking whips,
still splashes droplets of scarlet
across glowing white cotton blossoms hushed in the field,
still swings like lifeless fruit,
I cannot whistle along quiet acceptance,
this sick stomach is a different kind of red flag,
and these are two kind old men
but I cannot "look away, look away" anymore,
we must look history right in eyes,
and see all of the tears black mothers cry,
and I can smell a black church burning as they sing

Dixie,
that confederate anthem,
that left, right, left little jolly hooray,
boys, this is no longer the land of cotton,
and I know memory
is a hand you are reaching for in the dark,
but the crimes of man are not forgotten,
I know you'll "take a stand to live and die in Dixie,"
but your perspective on history is not
the only one that matters,
you see, black lives matter,
and I will not "look away, look away"
when another street is painted crimson
with the way blood spatters and pools
under a young black boy,
again, again,
no, I will not "look away, look away"
as neo-confederate flag rallies
are happening this weekend at
Walmart parking lots across the country,
no I will not "look away, look away"
because this country has done that
for much too long,
do not look away,
racism flies a new-old banner,
the KKK is recruiting young members,
and confederate flags are selling like bigoted hot-cakes,
do not look away,
do not look away,
look straight at it all, America,
do not flinch or avert your eyes.

How many more black bodies have to fall before we call it genocide?
How many more southern black churches must burn before we call it
    terrorism?
How many more black mothers' tears
have to ocean beneath our feet before we take a stand?
All I hear is DIE in dixie land.
All I hear is DIE in dixie land.

"In dixie land,
where a rebel flag flies,
and black boys die
or are locked in prison,
don't look away,
don't look away,
don't look away… anymore…"

⌘ Every Black Boy is a Lion

Cecil the African lion was hunted and killed in Zimbabwe in July 2015.
The world was outraged.

Every black boy
is a lion,
cub,
young little brave thing,
not quite the intrepid predator,
clumsy with unknowing,
thick paws tell what
he will become,
  (King)
heavy prints that his Legacy
makes in the heat of the sahara or the sidewalk
or the cracked asphalt of inner-whatever-city,
and someone will find fault in him,
always a trophy hunter with a badge
waiting for nightfall.

Every mama lion
knows the taste of tears,
licks the scruff
and tough mane
of her juvenile
black boy lion,
teaches him to growl
without
showing his teeth,
teaches him the smell of his own blood,
teaches him that Pride has many meanings
and each one can get him killed.

Every black boy is a Lion,
a lineage of power
stripped from grace,
if you haven't seen that resilience,

look a lion in the face,
another mother crying,
the safari is the streets,
if you don't think they're being hunted,
who are those people in white hooded sheets?

⌘ Presidential Tears

Every time
I type gun violence
on my new iPhone,
the autocorrect changes it
to fun violence,
because in 2016 there is
an autocorrect to our thoughts
that tries to stray us away from the truth,
there is an electronic veil
that keeps me from tasting
the metal under my tongue
from the wild gunfire
cracking open an asphalt night,
sidewalk chalk has a different meaning
when it has arms and legs and a head
with no face, and another body leaving
the world without a trace,
yesterday,
the President cried presidential tears
into the January 5th afternoon,
an executive order
was signed in the blood of too many names,
and today it is not as easy to buy an M-16 at your local Walmart
as it was yesterday,
because the President
is a man who has had enough,

yesterday,
the President shed tears
for Sandy Hook,
the first graders that are learning
their alphabet in the clouds,
and you would think
that a massacre of first graders
would stop this national crisis of guns,
but even the youngest and most innocent
have had no weight on all the horror that's been done,

and yesterday,
the president wiped away tears
for all of the children,
too many young black boys
who never became old black men,
and toy guns are just as deadly as the real thing especially
if you are 12 and black and playing make-believe on a playground,
and the police need policing,
and the mothers' grief needs releasing,
and it is all starting to bubble up into the throat of our leader,
the choke of a trigger has found the tipping point's needle,
and yesterday the President
cried the tears of a nation,
as a black man, as a father,
as the Commander in Chief
reaching frustration,
and when I saw those tears fall, I felt a change in the wind,
I see his presidential tears as a baptism,
a cleansing on the face of a dirty country,
his cheeks glistening with the last remnants of a history about to change,

yesterday,
the President cried Presidential tears,
and a poem my Facebook friend wrote about gunshots ripping apart
    classrooms
went viral on the internet,
there is a new canon of poetry
born of blood and bullets,
and the readers of the future
will look back on these literary
descriptions of our existence,
and I hope they will have no idea how to identify
this type of barbarism
in their real lives,
and when they type "gun violence"
into their holographic 8-dimensional iPhones,
the autocorrect will change it to
"fun violets"
or have no suggestions at all.

⌘ Driving to a Revolution

Let's just write the word LIGHT, poets.
I'll keep writing the word LIGHT.

If I got in my jeep this morning,
and drove 6 hours and 37 minutes northward,
I could stand on the front lines of a war,
a war that is one state away,
a war that only crosses one borderline,
I could taste the clouds of tear gas
still lingering like a heavy sin in the morning air,
I could hear the drones of helicopters and
armored cars, tanks tearing new veins into a city.

Let's just write the word LIGHT, poets.
I'll keep writing the word LIGHT.

If I just went out for a drive up the state to Ferguson, Missouri,
I could feel what war feels like in the afternoon heat,
I could know what it feels like to tie a t-shirt into a mask,
and Molotov the night with my own searching heart,
I could raise both hands up into the fiery sky,
open my palms to the universe, knowing I want LOVE not war,
I could hear what the cries of justice sound like chanting from
fed-up mouths, the music of frustration,
the reveille of a revolution waking up
and demanding that somebody answer for
another black boy down.

Let's just write the word LIGHT, poets.
I'll keep writing the word LIGHT.

This is our homeland insecurity,
this is the tipping point of mutiny
uprising in the streets of our native land,
there is no sand in our boots,
we are not overseas,
why are they sending the military disguised as police?
This is a peaceful protest that nobody wants you to believe.

The revolution will not be televised
because the government controls the feed,
and the media tries to control our minds,
they feed us eye for an eye until the whole world is blind.

Let's just write the word LIGHT, poets.
I'll keep writing the word LIGHT.

I did a peace meditation a couple of weeks ago.
During it, I envisioned every gun on the planet
turning into a long stemmed flower,
soldiers and police and criminals and hunters
wielding long stemmed tulips, roses, lilies, irises,
and every time they fired their guns,
their target would be hit only with petals,
thousands of colorful glorious petals,
and flower seeds would trace the trajectory,
falling onto the earth in a peaceful arch of
the promise of new life,
this was my meditation, just flowers,
every gun a long stemmed flower.

Let's just write the word LIGHT, poets.
I'll keep writing the word LIGHT.

If I get in my car tomorrow,
and if I drive just 6 hours and 37 minutes northward,
into a community of hesitant anarchy,
into a community that looks like Fallujah but is really Ferguson,
I will pack my jeep full of flowers,
and I will only speak the word
LIGHT,
and I know this is a revolution,
and I stand for what is right,
and I know this is a revolution,
but I am not here to fight.

Let's just write the word LIGHT, poets.

Let's just write the World LIGHT.

⌘ i FORGOT MY NAME

I forgot my own name once,
swallowed the aching words of so many women
that they became a dishcloth
lodged in my throat,
a muffle to my own mouth sounds,
and I was quick to judge myself,
unusual introversion,
what's wrong with me?
I'm not usually like this,
so inside,
so quiet,
a thrush blending into wood shadow,
conversations on repeat in my mind,
preventing my voice from finding the wet of night,
this much energy is not always a good thing,
being this sensitive, it hurts,
these eyes, these eyes
that see what everyone needs at all times,
these hands, these hands that only want to hold together
what is broken,
this heart, this heart that knows
too much is broken here,
this is a collection of sadness,
a gathering of shards under one fireside night, and
suddenly I forget my name,
because suddenly, I am all of these women gathered here,
I am the anxieties,
I am the self-harm,
I am the dark blue thoughts,
I am broken legs and the bruised arms,
I am the scarred wrists, the red waiting,
I am the depression,
I am the genderless shell of small child,
I am the abused wife,
I am the tears, and the shame, and the loveless game
rampant in this cluster of women,

too much pain in one place, and my spark is a diminishing flicker,
oh soul,
where is my light?
oh soul,
what is my name?

I forgot my own name once,
I tucked it underneath the ledge of someone's grief,
and slept for a hundred years.

Before the birds woke, I sang of morning,
I found my name in the trees,
my three letters carved on trunk belly,

K A I,

I found my name in the sunrise
blanket warmth of daybreak,

s K A I, sky,

breathe periwinkle rise,

I found my name
under the leaves of a century-old willow,
the way the light shone through her magical fronds,
swayback bends of branches
bringing me back to the center of my self,
the vibrations of earth, and green, and peace, and calm
whispered,

"You are here and everywhere, Kai.
You are here and everywhere."

⌘ Blood Moon

A blood moon rises,
my tongue swells
on the horizon of such heat,
such red worship,
my body in perigee
orbiting your heart
at its closest point,
paint the night
in the sun's shadowy ring,
crimson light falling
on my lips
as I howl your name
so the stars
can hear.

⌘ Fleeting

Another dream with your face,
your mouth swept across my sleep,
calling me closer to you in this realm
where bodies are only stars
and we can merge into a new spectrum,
your skin and its colors
folded into my astral projections,
my movement, gravitational,
pulling toward
the thumping whirl that you are,
heart, hands, voice, smile,
the light of me
finding the light of you
in this transient fleeting and forgetting,
I went to kiss your lips
and before I could touch them they were gone,
dandelion wisps floating away from my breath,
a wish I want to hold on to
but can never grasp,
you,
fleeting,
your lips,
fleeting,
like some unknown smoke
rising to tell a story that I will never hear,
painted grey in a night with no sounds.

⌘ Mahal Kita, Lola *(for my Grandmother)*

Tonight, I invoke all
of the love of my Ancestors,
as I try to write the
depth and strength and beauty
of my Lola into one poem.

How can I capture
a woman like Lola Senyang with only words?
Should I not include the sound
of banana leaves whispering her name in the wind?
Is she not the color of the sky at dusk,
when the sunset's golden beams paint
everything a warm pink glow?
How can these simple pen strokes
scratched onto a page
be enough for such a grand woman?

Grandmother.
When I think of you,
I think of a place I have
always wanted to go in my heart,
a place that has my name
written somewhere in the sand,
a place where my little girl
footprints left a story I
was to find 30 years later...
here, Calibungan, Victoria, Tarlac.
I did not know my own story,
but you've given me this gift,
Grandmother.

Your long and beautiful life
is woven like the finest leaves of anahaw
through the lives of so many people,
your story remains here, Lola,
it is the soil that makes the rice grow tall each year,

it is the strength of the caribous splitting the wet earth,
it is the laughter that echoes through generations,
it is the harvest,
the village,
the love.
Your hands form a woven
golden basket in the night sky,
holding the constellation of a cross over the farm
that glows 11 bright,
11 stars Dela Cruz,
the brightest star you hold for Lolo Basilio,
your true love, your magical reunion
unfolding in the heavens,
I saw you both glimmering last night
in the moonless sky.

10 more stars
in the woven golden basket
of your hands... your golden children
all with names of conquistadors or queens.

Jovita	*Each*
Josefina	*is*
Estrelita	*different*
Erlinda	*but*
Pacita	*together*
Francisco	*they*
Juan	*are*
Segundina	*all*
Jose	*the*
Mario	*same.*

You must be so proud of how brightly they shine, Lola,
how they lift each other up
and hold each other as ONE,
how each of them is warm and kind,
compassionate and hardworking,

strong and loving...
these are qualities only a mother and father
can show by example.

You are the Sun
that nourished each of them with your Light.
They carried your Light with them,
wherever in the world they went,
and passed that on to
another generation of the cross
    Dela Cruz
and that LIGHT will never stop growing,
passed to the young until they are old,
and passed to the young again.

Grandmother.
You were a Grand Mother,
the best mother raising a powerful tribe
of people who carry your gifts into the future.

I sit here today
observing as I write this,
your bodily-vessel lying in the adjoining room,
the flowers and light surrounding you,
the hum of angels and rosaries,
the constant parade of mourners
that have come here to pay you their respects,
the ones that knew Lola Senyang...

I have heard and seen
only beauty, music, laughter
and brief moments where grief outweighs it all.
The cries of your loved ones are temporary
for it is your SMILE that will carry us through losing you,
noble mother, kind grandmother,
Lola Senyang.

I wish I knew you better

when you were alive,
but I have learned more about you in these few days
than I ever imagined.
I feel you in the breeze
that relieves the oppressive heat.
I hear you in the voices
of the children as they play.
I hear you in the sounds of the morning,
the rooster, the sun peeking through quiet coconut palms.

I believe in the everlasting flight of the soul.
I know you are HOME now Lola,
not just in body, but in Spirit.

I can feel you in everything here,
I can see your hands in the midnight sky,
the family of stars you hold,
and if I close my eyes for a moment,
I can feel myself
turn to stardust,
the spark off a "little star,"
my mother,
Estrelita,
and tonight, I shine for you,
I shine as a spark in the giant
constellation of a cross over the farm,
a pattern of stars
        Dela Cruz
that the whole world can see.

Mahal Kita, Lola.

I love you.

⌘ How to be Fat and Beautiful

Don't look in the mirror,
unless you are looking with love.

Hug yourself,
pull in all the skin and flesh
so that a mountain forms
across your chest
from which a sun can rise.

Eat what you want to eat,
but also make yourself up into
a delectable meal,
a feast for the eyes
with colors and textures
and fragrances that captivate
all who see you.

Take selfies that make you feel sexy,
and share them on Facebook.

Wear clothes that show off your curves,
that highlight the swoop of your breasts,
the indentations of your body
where hands could go,
the invitation of flesh and bone,
and moving light swaying.

Sleep naked.

Find a lover who sees your beauty,
and listen to her when
she names you after volcanoes
and the summits of mountains.

Make love, be love, give love, take love.

Look people in the eyes
when they talk to you,
let them see down to your essence,
your spark, your ever glowing light.

Dance, even when you are embarrassed,
even when your body is not as fluid as your soul,
become water,
become a moving river,
dance until the ocean swells through you.

Touch yourself.
Take your own body into your own hands and
thank
every
glorious
cell,
hold every weighted ounce
until the gratitude you have
for your own body
makes you weightless,
names you flight.

Look in the mirror.
Smile, look into your own eyes without looking away,
love your reflection,
press your hand to the window of self,
kiss the glass.

Give yourself flowers.

When people say,
"you have such a beautiful face"
shout
"you should see me naked, I'm *gorgeous!*"

Cultivate your heart,
be kind, listen to people's problems,
help a neighbor, be compassionate.
Compassion is beautiful.

Break boundaries,
crush the ideals and standards of beauty
that society feeds us and eat from the wide banquet
of your own being.

Know that you are beautiful.
Order dessert. Enjoy every bite.

⌘ THANKS GIVING

being present,
being in the moment,
seeing the most in everything that comes my way
seeing the sacred in everything that crosses my path,
and hearing and experiencing only with
the most open heart,
the most open hands,
this is my thanksgiving,
this is giving thanks to the divine
that does not need a day to be celebrated,
because it is the energy,
the constant light source that we
are flowing toward in our constant striving,
in the ever-fluttering of our invisible wings.

⌘ How to Make a New Year's Resolution

The eve is here,
the cusp of a new beginning,
between the letting go and the taking in,
between the old habits and the new shaping,
the eve is here,
the time for new year's resolutions,
lose weight, exercise more,
budget your budget,
get that better job,
quit this, quit that,
change this about yourself,
work those hips, that shape, that physique
because you are not your best self now,
or at least that's what you are made to believe.

Make your new years resolution,
but I know that these cycles are just promises
we make to the breaking,
to the open chasms of our hearts
waiting to be filled with light,
this year,
I will not resolve to lose weight,
because the only time I really did lose weight
was not all the years that I hated my body,
hated the reflection of stretched out skin
and folds of unexplored softness, no,
the only time I really lost weight was when
I believed someone who told me I was beautiful,
when I saw that I AM Beautiful,
when you love yourself,
the beauty of your own higher self
fills in the cracks, fills in the empty.

If you want to exercise,
exercise your rights,
exercise your freedoms and stand for

the freedom of others,
exercise your voice,
speak up for the silenced,
hold a protest sign high in the air that proclaims
your own individual song into the night,
the buildings and windows and trees and sky
will ring in a brotherhood of repercussive chanting,
spirals of sound filling a chamber with human solidarity,
or exercise your tolerance for one humanity,
exercise harmony and compassion,
flex these muscles in the gym of your own
growing Spirit,
infinite mirrors that reflect
the weight of your Soul,
exercise your Spirit,
exercise the muscles in your face
that create a smile, that shape laughter,
exercise hugs, exercise peace.

You want to budget?
Budget quality time,
it's the only currency that matters.

You want to quit something?
Quit judging yourself,
quit judging others,
quit hate and separation,
quit building walls and start breaking them,
quit quitting on yourself and do something that
brings you joy,
when you have joy, share it,
quit keeping all the joy for yourself,
quit the people who bring you down,
quit accepting less than what you are worth,
you are golden, quit forgetting that.
This New Year's Eve,
make a wish upon the star
of your own beating heart,
hear the echo of that wish bounce

off the sun and back into your bones,
let's make this a New Year's Revolution,
let's make promises that serve others, not just ourselves,
let's bring in the new year
knowing everything is an open door, a chance,
a blessing, a teacher, a moment of decision,
a mirror reflecting infinity.
Happy New Year.

⌘ There Will Be An Orchard / I Throw Fruit into the Gully

I throw fruit into the gully,
when the oranges and apples
start to decay in the fruit bowl
of unintentional neglect,
I gather into my arms the
glorious seed
bombs
and I open the back door
that faces the gully,
the gully past the tulip patch,
the earth crevice for passing rainwater spillage,
the ignored river-let that leads to the stream, to the dream
that one day an orchard of mixed fruit will flourish.

I throw fruit into the gully,
over the past year or so,
one by one,
I lob the rotting produce
arcing colorful ovules of fruit
into the mouth of this green ravine,
the leftover 4th of July watermelon,
the jack-o-lantern whose smile
became a wilted frown,
a bundle of grapes,
black bananas,
anything that may decompose
and bury its seeds into the fertile earth
and occasional rainwater cascade.

I throw fruit into the gully,
some call this exercise fruitless, futile.
Now, I know I could plant the seeds,
carefully plot the land, and stand in the spaces
where the sun shines her full face,
but this is a gamble,

like putting it all on red,
like throwing pennies in a wishing well
and expecting that wish to become truth,
like wishing on a star
and waiting for it to flicker back
I hear you.

I throw fruit into the gully
because I have a bushel
of waiting tucked under my arm,
an abundance of hope collected in decay,
wishing these seeds into trees,
wishing these trees into an assorted orchard,
a motley bloom of cast out sprouts
becoming a majestic grove of

"why, yes this apple tree IS from the fruit I threw into the gully."

I throw fruit into the gully,
and yesterday,
walking down toward the lake,
at the end of the rainwater crevice
that reaches the stream,
where a pool of rich wet soil
has become a puddle of possibility,
there,
in all of its *accidental* glory,
a watermelon seed
is reaching
its tiny green arms
up out of the soil,
and becoming a miracle.

⌘ Grey Horse

Sometimes,
the urge to creak
back toward the numbness
returns,
a river running towards
a collapsed ocean,

Resist.

Perhaps,
I cannot stand
in the light
without remembering
the dark womb,
the sordid past that
built every stone I swallowed.

Inside me
a wall is being built
and torn down simultaneously,
a vacant shadow persists
and the music in my head
turns to silence,
impenetrable,
these are the demons
that sometimes still appear
attached to the ankles of my growth,
I try to shake them off,
the echoing noise of
wooden wind chimes,
bamboo hollow clip-clops,
a quiet stampede of grey horses
and their bodies of fog,
muffling hope.
I turn around
and face the stampede,
let the smoke and dissonance
run its course through me,
until the fog,
becomes water in my hand.

⌘ I Keep Going

I almost didn't make it to this moment.
When I was young,
about 11,
elementary school,
I had a macabre view
on life and death,
wished for my small life to end,
wished to defeat the fire in me
that had barely started to burn.
When I would get to school,
I would take a pen
and draw a dashed line
with a pair of open-mouthed scissors
eating the dashes like pac-man
on the inside of my left wrist,

- - - - - ✂< - - - - - - - - - -

Next to it,
I would write "cut on dotted line"
like
please, someone bleed me out,
let the red of this young body paint the playground,
instructions for self harm,
directions to my own eager destruction,
obviously, I wanted attention,
I wanted someone to ask me why?
I wanted someone to look into my sad eyes and
not dismiss my strangely penned plea.
I needed a friend,
someone to notice.

I kept going.

Depression held my hand for a long time,
she was a woman, and
I might have loved her once.
She came over me like a cloak
when I realized I was different, when I
noticed myself wanting to be close to the pretty girls,

how I wanted to kiss lips that were more like mine,
especially after my body was stolen from me at 13,
how his black hands led to the inescapable night of my soul,
how I was trained to believe that was I wrong for letting it happen,
an alien in my own body,
a criminal in the jail of adolescent fear,
my own silence covered everything like a dense fog,
and I knew the flavor of sadness,
of reaching for the unreachable,
of being in the closet
with God.

I kept going.

The last time
I attempted suicide
was when I was kicked out of the
Corps of Cadets,
a radically republican conservative military institution
that I joined in college,
in an effort to impress my father,
to become more like him, proud marine.
I was kicked out my junior year
for fraternizing with a woman in my outfit,
for falling in love with a girl,
violating the Don't Ask, Don't Tell policy,
and I really thought she loved me,
she let me take the fallout from the officers,
she let me take the harassment and the hazing,
she let me get expelled from the organization,
kicked out of my dorm, left alone with no one,
and how was I going to tell my mom?
I stayed with that girl for six more years,
because people who don't care about their lives,
don't care about their happiness.
I kept going.

Depression looks like drugs sometimes,
looks like stretching out for ecstasy
by swallowing pretty pills,

looks like a cloud of smoke
that never dissipates,
looks like the white rail of a train,
looks like opiate-induced blackness,
like falling, falling, falling into the darkest dark,
drug abuse was an escape
from everything that hurt,
was comfortable numbness
and almost death,
was two years of my twenties
that I don't remember as my life,
out of body, out of mind, out of soul, desperately aching.

I kept going.

Finally found my passion in teaching,
found a little solace in writing,
found the secrets that I held didn't have to be secrets forever.

My life has been
mostly shards formed back into whole,
light rising up and through stained glass windows,
painting everything with slants of color.
All that was dark
became the steps to my own illumination,
processing the pain
was the only way out and through it all,
writing it,
crying through it,
fighting through the masks that I desperately held onto,
punching at my shadows until they broke through to light.

My life has been mostly dark
because only those who walk in the dark see the stars,
I had to be able to recognize a star
when I saw her, my love,
when my soul woke up and said
"oh! she is here!"
when she walked through the threshold
of my collarbones and became one with me,

held a mirror up to my body
and named me *eternal*,
and all of my shadows were given wings,
and all of my shadows were given wings.

I keep going.

Flight

For once you have tasted flight you will walk the earth with your eyes turned skywards, for there you have been and there you will long to return.

Leonardo da Vinci

⌘ This Body

This body keeps spreading,
stretching like a flood
filling in space,
rolling out like muted dough
taut softness pull-pushing
wolf-hungry skin outwards
to some unknown corner of sky,
as if stars inside me await a natural birth,
supernova navel wishing flight,
this body,
gradual spilling over
into light-lack
places of shadow and ash,
becoming everyone
and everything in its path,
one and infinite,
one and everyone,
this body,
unfurl of grace lifted agony,
reflection spectrum of human being
that takes every step
into the glorious face of the sun,
this body,
fallen and risen,
fallen and risen,
sometimes dragged toward the vision
that I am *not* this body,
this physical vessel of flesh and bone,
I am a ten-thousand light beams expanding,
the universe is my home.

⌘ Metaphor

I looked up metaphor in the dictionary.
It spoke unclearly,
whispered a comparison that sounded like simile
but wasn't,
was more *is* and *are* and *being*,
the skylight blinking,
the moon humming a wet tune of tiding,
the murmuration of birds that my soul becomes
if I let it,
the hiding sun lifting an eclipsing veil
to reveal the glory of unbridled light in a smile over a desolate field at
    dawn,
this is metaphor
but I have not mingled in metaphor,
no, not in a while,
not since the last time I fell in love,
and falling felt like flying, not falling,
when I tripped and tumbled over the blazing hyperbole
of what our love was when
the fires inside were first lit by divine coincidence,
and the volcanic embers of our hearts' heat
could summon a wildfire from spark that
all the water in the ocean could not smite,
if the wind blew us right,
blew a breeze against her skin that reminded me
of what her kiss might feel like,
and that ember
would suddenly…ignite.

The poetic devices of love,
tools of expression that I wear like wings,
wings that never lose their feathers
or forget that falling

      can feel like flying

if you open yourself up and become a star.

⌘ THE HEARTS OF TREES (*for Kahig*)

A King once told me
about the hearts of trees.
They are what is left in the end,
when a tree is aged,
mostly fallen,
rotted with life and years,
solitary figure crumbling among tall brothers,
still,
husked in the decay of days,
there stands the heart of the tree,
a tall stalactite structure of wood ridges
and pulp tipping against the suggestion of wind,
but holding steadfast,
the inner sanctum of decomposing rings,
of woven circles erect in the balance of life and dying.

When I was a boy, I used to karate kick those down with all my might,
he said, pointing.
When I found out that was the heart of the tree,
I never kicked one down again.

I absorbed his delicate strength in the quiet wood,
his gift of saying so much with so few words,
his mastery over needless boyhood destruction,
long absolved by his compassion,
and we stood there in awe of a dwindling heart of pine,
strong pillar center of a giant,
beauty,
resonating forest memories,
evergreen,
even in its almost death,
musted,
layers broken,
long gone limbs,
peeled back face,
soft bark jackets strewn across warm pine-needle floor,

yet,
this heartwood remained standing,
jagged warrior through nature's waging battle,
tall as a King,
had it eyes, we would have looked in them level,
but we didn't,
we just both bowed quietly inside,
in a subtle respect for majesty,
the heart of a tree,
the heart of this Man,
both golden in the afternoon sun.

I could hear the heart beat of the forest
as we walked away in crunchy autumn steps,
leaving the proud remnant,
heart of a tree,
guarding the hillside with such grace.

⌘ A Million New Leaves

How can I not write about spring—
how the world outside
is slowly being enveloped in
this almost neon green newness,
this green that fills
in all the spaces
where naked limbs
taunted the landscape
with emptiness
and cold,
the winter months seemed endless,
but this green,
this neon birth of new leaves,
these flowering buds that throw
magentas and reds,
dogwood soft yellows,
and cherry blossom kisses
into the air with anticipation and wonder,
how can I not write about spring?

A whiff of Persian lilac wind
turns the corner and comes through
my window as I type, entrancing me
in my beloved's favorite scent,
the cardinal and chickadee
sit in the bird feeder
considering seeds,
hummingbirds circle in
quick spirals of tiny whirr,
and the ringing song of frogs
echoes in rounds the harmony of spring,
the levels of sound and color
and vibration needed to bring in a new season,
to signal all the seeds to start their arduous
journey up, up, up and out towards the sun,
to turn over a million new leaves,

and leave us with this feeling of hope,
of beginning again,
of planting seeds that you will
be around long enough to witness open,
and you, yourself become a sprouting
wonderful thing.

Outside, the neon green gently
quivers in the breeze,
the sun peaks through April's clouds,
an amplification of color.

It smells like rain.

⌘ Moving the Porch Swing

We moved the porch swing
to the other side of the house,
spring has opened up
a lush banquet of green,
the layers of cascading oak leaves
create shadows months long
where the porch swing was,
but now,
this warm two seater faces east,
is heated by the sunrise rays that pour
through tree openings and forest skylights,
invites me to swing my morning away,
back and forth,
back and forth,
a swaying spectator
to all that happens in nature's world
while we are inside on our computers,
but now I am out here,
swinging, mingling with winged things,
summer sits on the horizon,
waiting to dig her heels into the
recovering winter lawn,
the herbs in the garden box
poke their tiny seed heads up out of the soil,
promising seasons,
the dogs warm their furry bellies
on the soft deck boards,
sitting in slants of sun,
their wagging tongues dancing perspiration,
a hummingbird is preceded by its supersonic wing blur hum,
it flashes ruby and iridescent turquoise
preening itself on the twining vines of our jasmine
before realizing I am a silent witness
drinking in his colors,
drinking in the colors all around,
my cup of beauty,
this morning unfolding in green and sun and warm fur bellies,
and swinging back and forth, back and forth.

⌘ Morning Light

The only light
that comes into my space
is morning light
from the east,
the rising sun
beckoning me out
of bed to come to this
hallowed shrine of self
to pulse out letters
on this keyboard,
writing,
always writing,
this persistent companion,
this constant shadow
that lives in my mind
driving me to think in terms
of creative description,
forcing me to live
in this perpetual observation
of the world around me,
a great responsibility
to live as a quiet scribe
as humankind unfolds, creates, destroys,
and with all hope, creates again.

How can I properly report the vibrancy of a snail?
Illustrate the relationship of jasmine to the night air?
Chronicle the wingspan of a hummingbird's blurred flight?
Detail the myriad colors that make up each dusk?
How can I accurately catalog the emotional prism of Love?

The morning light
nudges me forward with each word,
I must portray our existence
for someone else to read,
future eyes

that are surely
inspecting the past
in search of Beauty,
among what I hope is not
our ruins.

⌘ An Open Letter to My Arm Flaps

Dear fleshy flaps of hanging fat under my arms,

Hey, you two.
How's it hanging?
Listen, I know we've had our differences,
and I really only loved you
when you disappeared for that year,
after I lost 100 pounds...
but don't worry, I found it again!
and there you are swinging wildly,
making my arms fit into dress shirt sleeves
like tight meat in sausage casings,
but I'm not hating you anymore, arm flaps,
no, I come today in humble reverence,
I'm on my portly-padded knees in gratitude.

I write this letter to lay a trail of
a thousand white gardenia petals
from my fingertips to armpits,
cave dwellings
with hanging rafters of fleshy weight waiting,
eaves of adipose tissue,
I think I would miss you,
if you were gone.
I want to lift you up,
move you like warm putty in my hands,
mold you into the shape of love.

I do love you.
Both of you.
You make the gentle quiet
of my embrace
a supple home for a lover,
a warm swaddle of skin and silk.

You are what makes my body an ample hideaway,
voluminous dwelling,
holy velvet waiting to fall.

Once hidden arm flaps,
I now consecrate you as *perfection*,
a resurrection from burden and shame
into soft glowing wings,
delicate undulations of wanting,
of pulling in,
of wrapping around
and holding close,
corpulent flags of beauty and plumpness,
glorious *wingspan*.

Yes, I name you my wings,
my low-hanging sails
that lead this body
across every moving ocean,
how you catch the swirling wind
and
suddenly,
we are flying.

⌘ Once in a Blue Moon

Once in a Blue Moon
take your clothes off outside
and meet the rising night,
remember how the air feels as
your only garment,
how your nipples
kiss the sky like a long lost lover,
dress yourself in only blue moon blue.

Once in a Blue Moon
run into someone's arms,
let them make you into a bird,
whirl you weightless into the circles
that make up every atom,
every cell,
every revolving planet that
revolves around your heart and her heart,
and fly, fly, fly.

Once in a Blue Moon,
look in the mirror
and ink the glass with fingerprints,
smudge your reflecting window
with how many parts you love about
your body, your glowing, glowing body,
point out the curves that sing,
the lines and folds that bless the body as shrine,
cursive script the word Beauty
over the glass echo of your face
and trace your shape in love, just LOVE.

Once in a Blue Moon,
look up at that glowing pale world,
that constant follower,
that moon silver wolf mouth,
and hear every poem of unrequited desire

that has been written under that
spectral waning waxing balloon,
and take all the words into your heart
like you are the YOU that every poem was written to.

Once in a Blue Moon.

⌘ LAMPLIGHT

The lamp
on my desk
just spoke to me
about defeat,
I was here to hear
the sound
of a bulb dying,
effulgence expiring,
a light collapsing on itself
and turning to quiet,
tiny coils cooling
in their dim new name.

I did not recognize
the hum of this light
until it burned out,
a quiet electric song
turning to
silence
and the corner
of my world
becoming
a request to be lit again...

so I bring my heart,
red and waiting,
and screw it
into lamplight socket
who begs for
threaded fullness,
and my heart becomes
a bulb of light,
tangible phosphorescence,
dazzle and gleam
reaching into the darkest corner
like I always knew it would.

⌘ CHANGING MY OWN NAME / KAI & KIMBERLY

(I've been lying to you. My real name is not Kai, but Kimberly.)

Kai means

willow tree in Navajo,
ocean in Hawaiian,
keeper of the keys in North Germanic,
victory and *open* in Chinese,
fire in Scottish,
strong and *unbreakable* in Burmese
in tagalog (my Filipino mother's mother tongue),
Kai means *friend*,
in Japanese,
ocean but also *shell* and also *forgiveness.*

Tonight, I forgive all the sins and shame
that came with my *first* first name,
the pain of a past life
lived out in this present one,
I died inside too many times to count but remained living,
the first 28 years of pre-soul-infusion,
existing in the illusion of ego and sleep,
the gathering of moments
that no child should keep,

yes, now my name has become a flame,
but started as a quiet wick
thatched and woven
by the hands of a mother who
only wanted a better life for her first born,
first child,
bright heart daughter,
I shall name you
Kimberly,
after Kimberly Clark,
who *must* be famous,

who *must* be successful,
who *must* have pockets lined with gold
since the worldwide distribution
of toilet paper dispensers
globally spread to the farthest reaches,
rolling out rolls and rolls
of toilet paper
to wipe up the shit of humanity,
to wipe up the shit of humanity,
to wipe up the shit of humanity,
WAIT!

That is not what she meant,
it was the glory of the name to an
immigrant farm girl clinging
to the illusion of
what looks like prosperity,
what looks like fruition,
and I was the gift waiting to fall
into a name I could grow into triumph.

My mother read an article about Kimberly Clark
when she was in her twenties,
working at Clark Air-force Base in the Philippines,
dreaming of her own wings,
dreaming of escaping a life that
she knew was not big enough for a woman like her,
and that name stayed in her memory
until I was born,
western facing daughter,
with a name lined in a mother's beautiful hopes.

I once asked my father
many years later,
why Kimberly?
He said only… *Diamonds,*
there is a diamond mine in South Africa
that holds my name in its teeth,
and my daddy knew deep down
that a black coal

can still become something that shines,
but
Kimberly,
Kimberly turned to Kim,
turned to dim,
and over the years the light faded
from behind my eyes.

Kimberly
means *grey* in America,
means *suicidal tendencies* in America,
means *addiction as escapism* in America,
means *eat all your fucking feelings* in America
means *don't ask don't tell* in America,
means *all the dark things that made up Kim* in America.

Yes, I ended up with more shit than glory,
more dark than diamond,
more coal and calamity
than anything that shines,
and to no fault of dear mother,
shit happens,
and I was some kind of litmus-shitmus test,
dipped in too many painful experiences
for one growing girl.

Somewhere, there is also a *royal meadow*,
and that's where the name
Kimberly historically is derived, from the *royal meadow*.

Kimberly,
I left her in that meadow long ago,
but today I will close my eyes,
I will go to that abandoned field of memory
and I will meet her face to face,
I will pull her broken large body close to me,
hold her until her walls crumble into ash,
rest her head on the unbreakable collarbone of KAI,
and
call *Kimberly*... friend.

All will be forgotten,
all will be forgiven,
all will bend
like a laden willow,
and the empty shell of a girl
will open
to be filled
with an ocean.

⌘ Alive in a Thousand Places

At this moment,
I'm alive in a thousand places,
myriad forms of self,
scattered like dandelion florets
spinning in the breath of a nameless wind,
filling up the spaces of someone's thought
or someone's faint memory
of me.

He remembers me as the teenager
in the black Metallica t-shirt
chain wallet slapping the outside of my thick thigh,
blue jean rips spelling movement and too much growth,
sneaking cigarettes into church camp in gutted out markers.
That was 20 years ago,
but I live as his best friend, that girl, in his mind.

She remembers me as her favorite teacher,
how she laughed in my class every day,
how she could really trust me to understand her,
and writing might just save her from
having the same fate as her dead brother,
and maybe prison will never know her name.
There is always a pedestal under me
in her remembrance and she carries me like a torch
into her growing up to woman.

Mom prays for me every night,
holds my heart in her hands and
sends wishes on stars all the way to my dreams,
she worries, she remembers every mistake
and every heartbreak that carved my face from stone,
worries I am not making the most out of my life,
worries I might not be eating right, or brushing my teeth,
or how I will ever have a baby, if I still live with a woman.
She holds me as daughter, forever,

living in her consciousness as a somewhat broken child,
though now, as a woman, I shine.

Each life I have colored
has a lingering touch of who I am,
who I was, who I remember being
to each individual I encountered.
There are hundreds of others.
They are not all thinking of me right now,
or maybe they are.
Time is not the linear constraint
people seem to think it is;
it is cyclical,
every moment at once,
it is fluid,
melting,
merging into other moments,
just as the definition of self
cannot be held down by the thumb of right now.

I am alive in thousand places,
I am made up of parts of me
that are the thoughts of every person
who thinks of me,
how she remembers my hands and their strength,
how he knows what holds my laughter,
how my lover can tell I am crumbling,
every person who hears my poems and holds me against my words,
every person who learns something from me and teaches me,
every person who
loved me,
made love to me,
held me,
broke me,
found me,
loved me whole again.

I am alive in a thousand thoughts.

I am scattered in the wind of those thoughts,
the continuum of my existence,
the fluidity of my beingness,

the stained glass window of my soul that soaks in the
magnificent sunrise and leaves colors, brilliant, over everything I touch...
and in the darkness of night, becomes a quiet deeper peace that echoes
    into the silence.

At this moment
I'm alive in a thousand places. So are you.

⌘ Photographing an Expectant Mother
(for Hope)

She is
almost
burst
-ing,

a sun

glowing
heavy light,
woman
holding life
inside a womb
that I try to capture
with the curve of my lens
with the curve of her body
against the backlighting day,
how her over - arching middle
becomes the only focal point,
how her open hands already
form a cradle and a moon
rocking still quiet waves,
and I can almost see
the baby smiling.

⌘ Twilight, A Study

The sky is over my shoulder,
I can hear her breathing on my neck,
whispering something about change,
something about morning that tastes like beginning.
I have been a friend to the morning,
welcomed the angles of light pouring
down on all that stands to face the day,
every tree that continues this perpetual reaching
and growing, and spreading, and falling.

There is a ritual that comes with morning and trees,
how each leaf has its turn to shine,
to become gold-leaf exaltation triumphant fire,
even for just a second,
then another day full of green,
as the scurry of birds feeding and creatures foraging
creates a hum of movement,
a musical chorus of life that welcomes the day.

Morning.
Do these creatures wake up from nights of dreaming?
Do birds dream of walking as much as I dream of flight?
Each song is different,
but I know they all sing about the same thing,
this song of being alive,
this tune that gets stuck in my throat sometimes,
hides under my tongue in momentary forgetting,
that I should be singing, should be greeting the morning
with a song of thanks,
and today I hear it,
rising with the gentle sun,
making its way across the stretched out limbs and branches,
lighting every thirsty blade and calm stone.

Morning is an in-between time,
a time that bleeds from darkness into day,

a merging of two worlds,
a cycle that never stops, reliant sun, constant traveler.

Twilight is another in-between time,
a time that bleeds day into night,
a moment that I took for granted until I sat on the deck
and watched as the skyline of trees began to change,
as the sky's color began to fade,
the sun on the precipice of falling behind the horizon once again.

This was not an exceptional twilight,
just magical in its regularness,
just everything beautiful in its casual changing,
the merging of worlds,
the sky blue subtly losing its colors to time,
the trees changing to only silhouettes
against a backdrop of fading day,
they become forms in only negative space,
the light behind them giving them definition in opposites,
every leaf, limb, branch, moving swaying wing of green
painted in the blackness of silhouette and shadow.

I had not given much thought to the in-between of twilight,
to the gradual fading that we often miss
when the world is almost dark.
There is magic there,
there is a play of light
that pulls out a sense of magic and discovery,
the fireflies of summer dance their light stories
during the mystery of twilight,
harbingers of fantasy that paint the night with their bodies.

Hold my body
against the fading blue sky day,
watch as my limbs and curves become
a blackness that is still me,
the negative space of my being against the light,
the silhouette that my shape makes against the coming of night.

⌘ Mona Lisa, A Study

Quintessential beauty,
you are the foreground
of a landscape that winds and blurs,
a scene that escapes breath
lest the sun sets across your placid shoulder,
buttercream skin,
ivory, porcelain,
all the words that convey
this off-white perfection.

I become the winding road
that leads to the softness,
the winter haze of your bosom,
the northern cross of your plump hands
and rose-dipped fingers.

I become every inch of painted sky
that outlines the folds and flowing curls
of your red brown blanketed hair,
the thin, almost invisible veil on your goddess head
that keeps me from folding into you with my mind.

Oh, Mona Lisa.
Oh, Juliet of the paint,
unrequited muse of da Vinci desire,
what secrets are you holding
on the delicate half-smile,
those borderline-sleep eyes,
that towering straight nose, I suppose
I would only hope to touch your skin,
to unveil the mysteries of lust and sin
that clothe you so well in this seeming nonchalance,
your brilliant dullness,
your radiant silence,
your demure wanting.

Oh, Mona Lisa,
tell me your secrets.
You have a voice that needs no sound,
a knowing that makes men fall to their knees,
a face that is a mirror and the wide open sky,
beauty,
myth,
beauty,
love,
make me a pure clean canvas
that I might stand in front of your light,
I will become the shadows,
the mask,
the depth of artistic portrayal,
blank as your mouth,
as the vision of enduring passion,
this empty fullness,
those eyes that follow me
to the darkest of nights
and become
two piercing stars.

⌘ If By…

If by "goodbye,"
you mean
come back to the beauty that we had before this escaping, this falling,
then I say hello.

If by "forgive me,"
you mean
let's sweep up all the pieces that I left broken at your feet,
then I forgive you.

If by "I'm sorry,"
you mean
take this tooth and nail, and with it build the semblance of wings,
then I am sorry, too.

If by "thank you,"
you mean
my shadows have turned to gold, and the dawn no longer fades from my
    mouth,
then you are welcome.

If by "I love you,"
you mean
there is an opening in a wall that only my light can sing through,
then I sing I love you, too.

If words are like actions completed in our minds,
let my words only be sunrises,
let my words only be green with spring,
let my thoughts only sound like rivers returning home,
let my desires only be the filling up of a cup that we both make with our
    hands,
let my actions only be the reflection of the sun on the surface of a
    rippling lake,
so bright, it illumines the underground of my being.

⌘ Line

Line of sight
is not a substitute for love,
but
I love you
and if looking at you is all that I can do,
then keep me in line with your mouth,
with your firefly eyes
speaking to me in the not speaking that we share,
keep me in line with your hands,
and I will point all of my fingers toward your palms,
only wishing I could be held in them but once,
just kissed
and swallowed
and breathed in with your lips,
keep me in line with your axis of yearning,
be my truest true north,
my magnet's hard arrow spin,
hold me in this malleable place grounded with nothing
but your heart beat,
I will put my ear to the dirt and
find the fine dust of your name,
the footprints of where I once stood in your shoes.
I will stand in this love
until my feet know
they only want to walk in circles
toward you.

Love, keep me in line with you,
take a string and tie it around my finger,
tie the other end to your ear
and hear me tap out your love letters in quiet morse,
these poems speak for themselves,
it is clear that I love you.
But never having you to love,
this constant wanting and never having,
this constant looking but not touching,

this aching to be filled,
is all that keeps me in this silly game,
cat and mouse chase of hearts
that do not know
they are already home and need not run.

Keep me in line with you,
make me point B to your point A,
give me a point to be, a purpose,
a reason to see the world in strokes of love
and gentleness,
and quiet,
and longing,
the shortest distance between us is still much farther than I can take.

I have spent decadent lifetimes waiting to be yours,
waiting to be in line to the throne of your mouth,
abdicate your seat of silence,
make me royalty, love,
paint me in the deepest purples
so the only color that resounds next to me
is the gold of your majestic heart.

We will be Queens of the Heavenly Bodies
our bodies make together in love,
space,
and bends,
and arcs,
lines in the night
tracing constellations of light.

⌘ Firefly

Poetry is in moments
written
in
  the
   air
as they unfold,
glimpses of universal perfection,
instances of your face meeting God,
when the movement and swirling of everything
traveling from everywhere

stops

for
a split second,

and I can capture the poem in it,
fluttering and flailing no more,
just still and present light,
a captured firefly
in the mason jar of my mind,
held and studied under the curvature of glass,
magnification arcing mirrors and wonder,
until its wings start to twitch

and the light,

      the poem

         is set

           free.

⌘ Saving My Mother's Voice
(for my mother, Ester Coggin)

I can't bring myself to delete
my mom's voicemail messages,
this has been going on for about a year now,
when she calls me, and I miss it,
there is always that little knowing
that I will still hear her voice,
she still shoots her love like a glittering star,
like a wild-heart comet
that narrowly misses my ear,
until I see it later,
one voicemail and one missed call
from Mom Coggin.

I can't bring myself to delete
my mom's voicemail messages,
the ones that almost all sound like this
(in her really strong little Filipino accent)

"Hi, Kimberly, where are yooouuu?
Can you call mommy back?
Okay, I love you."
or
"Hi, Kai.. what are you doing?
Okay, this is mommy.
I love you."
or
"Hoy…. what is GOING on?
Okay, love you. This is mom. Hope you're okay"

She always makes sure to tell me it is her,
like I don't know her voice shaped me from the hemline of angels.

This growing collection of 11–15 second
sound-bytes of love,
this compilation of a mother's worry,

a mother's missing,
a mother's reaching,
they stack up on my phone like a house of cards reaching the sky,
and I can't ever see myself pushing it over
with the delete button,
scattering the sounds to the wind.

When my gigabytes started dwindling,
I had to get an app to take the messages off my iPhone
and transfer them onto a folder on my computer
called "Mom's Voice."

Mom's Voice...
because, God forbid, if something ever happens to her...
at least I can hear...
and even though I know she is not going anywhere
anytime soon, if I can help it,
you just never know...
the hands of fate are impetuous,
and the Universe works in mysterious ways,
and damn it if there is not
a closed up fist of guilt in my heart
for all those times I didn't call her back
when I was struggling through the cocoon
of forging my own path, and losing myself and finding myself again,
all those times I didn't answer because
my life was not something that I wanted to TALK about,
my lover was not someone that I could *weave* into the conversation,
and hiding had become such second nature,
that it became this numb acceptance.

I call her back every time now.
As a woman, I can empathize with the aching
of a mother's heart,
the worry she feels when her kid is
at college and she can feel that something is just   not   right,
but her kid won't answer the damn phone!
I would go crazy,
I call her back every time now.

When I went to visit her over Christmas,
I noticed she still had the same house phone from
like 12 years ago, and it wasn't working right anymore.
My voice was still the answering machine's voice
when someone called the house, saying,
"You have reached 281-498-4261, please leave us a message
and we'll give you a call back as soon as possible.
Thank you and have a nice day,"
even though I hadn't lived there in almost ten years.
It was time for an upgrade.
We went and bought her a new model and
I unplugged the old and installed the new.
I asked her if it was okay to just throw away the old one
and she said sure, so I did.

The next day, my sister, mom and I
sat around the dinner table looking at old photos
and reminiscing, and this look of shock appeared on her face.

"Oh my god, where are all my messages?"

"What do you mean, mom?"

"Oh, no… we threw away all my messages…"

Just like me,
she had hoarded the voices of loved ones,
little sound-bytes of love that she had collected
on the old tape of the answering machine,
skipping their erasure every time,
deleting the creditors that still call the house for me,
and the mundane calls from friends,
but for years, saving this collection of everything dear,
this love collage she could play back when the empty house
was a little too empty,
and I had thrown the answering machine away,
and the garbage truck came that morning,
and all of those voices…
all of that encapsulated love, her (now dead) mother's voice,

relatives in the Philippines calling from the farm,
holiday calls from Canada where her brothers and sisters live now,
calls from my sister and me, all wiped away, vanished, scattered to the
    wind.

I started crying,
thinking of the "Mom's Voice" folder
I had just made on my computer before this trip,
and I could only imagine the thought of its accidental deletion.

"When I couldn't find you for all those months,
and you wouldn't call me back, I always just pushed
the button and listen to your voice, and say
where are you daughter, where is my Kimberly?"

"I am here now, mom."

We wiped our tears,
I told her that I do the same thing
with her messages, and we laughed
seeing how deeply similar we are,
how her golden thread is kite string straight
to my heart, how messages are just reaching,
and reaching is love's unfurling beacon,
a reminder, a promise, unending.

On the morning before my flight out,
she had to work, and I saw her off with hugs and kisses in the driveway.
I decided to set up her new answering machine.
I recorded the outgoing message with a new compassion in my voice,
that though I don't call this home anymore,
there is always a part of me that lives here,
a sound-byte that resonates here,
an echo of love that bounces off the walls of my memory.

After recording the message,
I called the house phone to make sure it worked.
I left her the first voice message on her new answering machine,
and passed the phone to my sister and her husband

and we all told her how much we love her,
and Merry Christmas and Happy New Year,
and I smiled inside knowing
this would be the sweetest surprise when she
got back from work that evening.

It was a full circle,
meaningful and beautiful.

I can close my eyes at any time
and hear my mom's voice,
but I still save her messages on my phone,
and I bet, if I checked her answering machine today,
there would be voice messages stacking up, up, up,
like a house of cards reaching the sky.

"Hi Kai... this is mommy. I love you."

⌘ THREE-FEET-AWAY (*for my sister, Diana*)

There are 21 days
out of every year
where I am only
one year older than you, little sister,
but there are centuries
and lifetimes
where our bond has been
created from gold and stardust
and the water that fills up clouds,
effervescent and rising,
we continue to find each other,
hold tight like magnets,
sometimes opposite poles
but always on the axis of love,
nothing is closer than a sister,
nothing could fill up my heart more
than the memories we have shared together
in this dance of karma and connection,
in this triangle of flame
we share as a family,
three women,
one right angle mother
and two 45° angels striving
to become that whole perfection that she is,
when one of us dims,
the others fight to light her again,
and I want to say it clearly now,
if finding myself ever made a sister-shaped hole in your heart,
I am only sorry for the moments of closeness we missed.
If you love someone, let her go,
if she returns, she is yours forever,
remember, sister, I am yours forever,
whole now, and shining,
and our hearts are filled with sister-shaped fullness.
There is nothing closer than a sister,
except maybe a shadow,

perhaps that is why I have never written a poem about you,
you are not an other,
you are not outside of me,
no observations needed on someone so familiar,
for we are fruit of the same vine,
our experiences so intertwined that
they are the same story with different voices,
and the ebb and flow of our lives has always been
on the same ocean,
the shore,
always our tender hearts.

We have always had each other's backs,
been each other's confidant
when everything was breaking,
in our twin beds three feet apart,
this whisper closeness,
you were the stable little lamplight love-source,
the follower who always wanted to be with me,
when I felt like no-one really did,
you were the one in the matching polka dot outfit mom made us wear,
the one who would race for the front seat,
and the (now hilarious) food racing competitor,
the dish rinser to my dish scrubbing,
the other latchkey kid,
the "get off the phone!"
the way we will always laugh at the same things,
the walk to school and back home together,
the slumber parties and McDonald's birthdays,
the countless Filipino gatherings where we
were our only form of entertainment,
the "my best friend had to have a little sister
so we could all play together"
the church groups, and team sports, the after school,
the swim team and how you were awesome
and I could never dive even after 8 years,
the "stay on your side of the room!"
the "shut up!" "you shut up!"
the "Mom, Diana scratched me"

the "Mom, Kim punched me"
the "stay on your side of the room!"
this three feet away closeness,
always there, little sister,
until I left for college,
left for life,
and you left for college,
travelled the globe push-pinning continents,
left for life,
and we saw how that physical closeness
built such a love between us that it is forever unbreakable.
Forever.
Unbreakable.

Diana,
I gave you your name,
I pulled it out of the sky and
wrapped it around your life
like a cloak of protection,
and maybe it was because Princess Diana
was so pretty on TV,
or maybe sometimes a young big sister soul can see
far into the future without knowing,
Diana means "heavenly, divine"
but Diana is also
Goddess of the hunt, forests,
and childbirth,
and maybe there was a call made
from a big sister to a Goddess
on a Bangkok December day in 1981,
asking for a shield to be given,
asking for a star to be held tight in the firmament,
because in the future, there would be a Diana
who wished for nothing more than to be a mother,
and the Goddess would remember the call,
and remember the little star holding an X in his tiny hands,
she would whirl him into form and flesh
and lay him gently into your warm and open arms,
and maybe that is the power a name can give,

Diana,
sister,
now mother,
and maybe big sisters can make stars fall down to earth to you.

Today,
it's your birthday
and I am only one year older than you for the next 21 days
there are 5,688 miles
one ocean and a couple of seas
between us,
but I have never felt closer to you,
I have never felt a sweeter love than the level
of three-feet-away closeness I have for you now,
as we are both grown women
knowing that the love of a sister
is an intimacy that is
created from gold and stardust
and the water that fills up clouds,
effervescent and rising,
to meet you
where
your heart is.

⌘ Dad & The Dalai Lama *(for my father, Dan Coggin)*

"The Dalai Lama told TIME Correspondent Dan Coggin, who journeyed to the god-king's exile in the Indian Himalayas at Dharamsala, that 'Tibet still exists despite all the Chinese have done. But I don't know for how long. Another 20 years like this and there will be no Tibet.'"

(DAN COGGIN, *Tibet: Himalayan Hell*, September 13, 1968. TIME)

What was it like, dad?
These quiet heroics
of which you never spoke,
these moments
that would have shaped you
out to be more of a man
in our eyes, than the man you were,
this past that built you
and broke you
before we were even born,
why didn't we know you?

I found out more about you
after you died than
I ever knew of you when
you were alive.

There were too may wars
tucked into the bags under your eyes,
too many of your CIA secrets
to distinguish the truth from the lies,
and I know you couldn't
sleep for the last
30 years for your life,
but this was just the beginning,
the early stages
of your renegade reporting,
the beginning of a career
surmounting impossible obstacles
to get to the story,

dad,
what was this moment like?

Young American reporter, Dan Coggin
Young exiled Tibetan God-King, His Holiness the Dalai Lama,
33 and 33,
both born in 1935,
both men of honor,
of spirituality,
of broad views,
both peaceful hearts,
two men becoming,
dare I say, brothers? friends?
or just an interviewer and a story?

September,
what was the weather like in September,
in Dharamsala, India,
in the Temple of His Holiness, dad?
Was there a mountain under your feet?
Were there a million stairs that led upwards infinitely?
I know you took pictures,
you were a photojournalist,
and if I'm anything like you,
I know you took pictures, dad,
where are the pictures?
Why do I keep having to prove to myself
that my dad was a hero,
over and over,
in all these different languages?

What did you wear to the interview at the Temple that day?
Did you wrap yourself in robes,
or were you the bellbottom-business class American?
I keep painting the scene in my mind,
the wide open room,
the vibrant colors, red and yellow walls,
shaved heads of young Tibetan monks
in russet robes,
the heavy smoke of sandalwood permeating

the sacred space all around
painting thick the holy,
and they let you in, dad.
Why?
The Dalai Lama let you in
to hear the plight of Tibetans from his lips,
and he trusted you to convey his plea
for the most widely published American magazine,
and all I keep wondering about
is those little details,
like did you use that little gold pen?
Did your left-handed script scribble down
every word, or did you listen with your eyes and heart,
did he trust you from the start,
or did you build something
with the storylines of your young brave face?

All I keep wondering about is
did the steam rising from his tea
fog up his black framed glasses, dad?
And did he grin? Laugh?
Did you both laugh?
Did you make him comfortable?
I bet you made him comfortable,
in his Temple, somehow you
extended your compassionate heart,
and he opened like a White Lotus to you,
you heard the stories of his
300,000 Tibetan people exterminated,
still more jumping into the Kyichu river,
(the River of Happiness)
to commit suicide as proud Tibetans
rather than suffer under Chinese control.

You must have sipped your tea
so gently
as he told you of the
1300-year-old statue of Avalokiteshvara,
the eleven-headed Buddhist God of Mercy,
smashed by Red Guards

and thrown into a gutter with
burning sutras and tantric scriptures crumbling into ash,
dad,
how did your heart become this depository of
the world's pain?

Did you know then that you were also exiled?
That you were a young man
from Atlanta, Georgia,
who would spend the better part of his life
in Asia, telling the horror stories
of wars that were not yours to witness, dad?
Korea, as the youngest sergeant in the Marines, 18,
oh, how your blue eyes must have cried at all they'd seen,
then as a journalist in
Vietnam.
Tibet.
Cambodia.
Thailand.
Pakistan
and what surely pushed you to the extremes,
the 1971 Atrocities in Bangladesh,

TIME MAGAZINE: A Letter From The Publisher, August. 2, 1971

DAN COGGIN *has spent most of the past seven years observing turmoil in
Asia—grim but invaluable experience for his latest assignment, this week's
cover story on Pakistan. A former Marine, Coggin witnessed the Indonesian
crisis of the mid–'60s, went next to South Viet Nam and then served as New
Delhi bureau chief. Assigned to the Beirut bureau last fall, he continues to
contribute his expertise on Pakistan. He was one of the 35 newsmen expelled
from Dacca on March 26, but in April he trekked from India by oxcart,
rowboat, motorcycle, bicycle and bus to become the first American journalist
to get back to the Eastern capital. He returned again for this week's story and,
despite his having seen much war in the past, found that "this one has special
horrors."*

special horrors,
oh dad…

all before I was born.

It was after your death in 2012,
that I have reached out to reporters,
historians, professors in Bangladesh
who know the name Dan Coggin,
American Journalist,
Hero to the Liberation War,
your name stands like its own flag.

I found out that,
as a journalist,
you made a career
of getting Kings
and Sheikhs,
Prime-Ministers
and Presidents
to tell you their stories,
to confess their humanity,
why didn't you tell me your story, dad?

On that day in 1968,
with His Holiness the Dali Lama,
in that remote Temple
in Dharamsala,
did sweat roll down
your fervent brow,
as the spiraling tea steam rose
into your blue sky eyes?

Dad,
looking across the table
to that god-king man,
that exiled brother,
did you stay inside yourself,
or did you look up through the steam and
smile?

⌘ Visiting A Stone

Visiting a stone
with your name on it,
ashes collected underneath,
remains,
makes no sense to me.

You are not there.
You are everywhere.

But I understand the physicality of grieving,
the call back to the body that is left behind,
how everyday there is a void.
a need for touch, tangibility,
longing.
Carefully placed flowers shooting up,
every petal saying, "he loves me, he loves me..."
freshly mowed grass
and names of other soldiers.

The wife who wonders what to cook for dinner
for the memory of you.
I understand the touchstone that, for her,
momentarily bridges the chasm between worlds,
fills the space you left behind.
By going,
she knows, "he loves me, he loves me..."
and I place another flower by your name written in stone,
and kiss the sky where you live.

⌘ Talk to Me

Talk to me with leaves in your hair,
tell me where you have been,
tell me that I am not a stranger
and that you have known my face for years,
would recognize it anywhere,
especially in the dark,
I am remembering the way that
you move, the way that the horizon eats the sun,
in these infinite circles,
I'll move with you, follow the
fireflies as they rise from your heated light.

Talk to me, only with your hands,
sign my name with your fingers so that I can hear it,
finger-point write the word love in cursive across the air,
love, love, love, your ups and downs,
make touch a sound,
make touch a sound,
we can make the quietest loud.

Talk to me with moonlight on your lips,
there is a star on my tongue
searching for a constellation to join,
I see you only in pinpricks of light shining through skin,
let our stars collide,
I will only stare into your eyes
until the light of our crash hits the earth,
and time bends toward our arching bodies.

Talk to me when your feet are wet,
when you are a dripping puddle of a woman,
and you only need my hands
to wring you out
and wring you in,
twist infinities into your hair
and lap up your rainwater mouth,
leave me with small pools of you and
I will swallow you into vapor.

⌘ Becoming Vapor and Rain

"I want to do with you what spring does to the cherry trees."—Pablo Neruda

Coax
you open
with soft color,
pull you back from
winter's dead lips,
you are naked,
stripped
and I will warm you
with the sun
I hold on my brow-line,
fire that wants to burn your name
into the hips of the earth.

I offer you
this open heart,
bury it
underneath
your branches,
until I root
into your roots,
until we tangle
into forests of wanting
into a system of knowing
what only we know,
nourish,
soil,
earth,
mouth,

dear love,
I want to crack open the sky
with my tongue against the breeze,
I will be a cloud
that follows you to the ocean,

a loyal fog,
be the river that meets me there,
and we will merge,
make a beautiful steam,
evaporation of desire,
evanescence of impulse and lust,
we will rise as vapor together
into the mouth of blue,
we will come down
like rain,
our atoms,
our bodies,
becoming joined water,
filling all the empty hollows with our deluge,
making pools that reflect the moon,
this is union, love.

This is how I found you
when all I had
was the taste of wanting on my lips,
I followed the water,
I flowed into everything
until you floated up into me,
you are my budding hope opening,
blossom of all that is beauty,
heat,
heat,
we will rise like heat
into the upward draft of zephyrs,
and there
we will carry on this dance,
this perpetual cycle
of becoming lifted vapor and gentle rain,
rising and falling
like the heaving, breathing earth,
making everything wet and new with our love.

⌘ You Become Me Become You

"Does the cosmic space, we dissolve into, taste of us then?"—RILKE, THE
SECOND ELEGY

On a night
of playing checkers and laughing,
we exchange cloud-filled breath
into the frog-crooning night,
the air hints at summer,
the window is wide open,
both to our living room
and to this higher realm
beyond the mental body,
this place where the soul speaks
beyond the footfalls
of self-effacing questions,
we are mountains trading hearts,
there is freedom in the way
we swirl around each other in flight,
fading into and out of.

In passing conversation,
you randomly recite the words
of a poem that I wrote hours ago
without ever reading it,
you use the *exact* phrases,
almost line by line,
talk about roots tangling,
and forests of trees,
and ripping open spring cherry blossoms,
and you say it all with the same wild wanting
I used when I wrote the poem
and I say, laughing,
*"You just said the exact words
of the poem I wrote this morning!"*
And we both know what it means—
you are so attuned

to my heart,
that I need not dwell
on *"how did you do that?"*

You
become
my thoughts
and
the words
I hold inside
resonate through you
like your body is a cave
and your mouth is my echo.

I know the priceless reality
of this love,
we have become one,
not in the traditional sense,
not in the sense of I do's,
but in the sense of reds and blues
glowing into healing purple,
in the sense of this is my broken shell,
fill me with all your light,
in the sense of I will stand by you,
with my sword ready to fight,
just so you can remember your own grace,
in the sense of you will never be lonely
and I will never be far,
I am the universe gifted to you,
and you are the universe gifted to me.

I have felt
the warmth of infinity
on your lips
and burst
into a new born star,
showering fire blue light
into dark ever-expanding space,
you have danced a swirling trail of supernovas
that reaches through countless millennia
and become every Queen at once.
I can taste the stardust
on your teeth.

⌘ Freak

When we met,
your first words to me
were across the threshold door
of a crack house,
you were giving a chiropractic treatment
and I was delivering the news of winning
Teacher of the Year to my best friend
(girlfriend of said crack house inhabitant),
and the stars had aligned
in such a way that our souls could possibly
have some kind of laugh at circumstance,
I knocked
and you answered,
opened the door and said,
"Hey Freak"
because you thought I was someone else,
"Nice to meet you, too,"
I answered,
you blushed
and I brushed by you,
and that was that,
the unromantic beginning
to a love that knows only the bounds of infinity,
the ever reaching outward
all-knowing omnipotence of this meeting of our hearts,
as though we had put
a bookmark on this love affair,
and I was there,
walking through a door
held open by you,
that may have been the door to my own becoming,
and I had to die
to find the strength to walk past that proverbial doorframe
and enter the unknown with you,
my beloved,
my infinitely opening woman,

and by that night,
I was reading you a poem over the phone
and you were already the muse I knew was mine,
and we loved and we loved.

It has been 8 years now of
blending opposites
into different shades
of wonderful,
different strokes of,
my god, I *do* love you...

What I think of now
is what might happen when I lose you,
how a 30 year head-start to life
you have
over me
will result in sorrow
when we reach your finish line together,
and oh, how you have taught me to cheer you on
at that finish,
that crossing over threshold
to the other worlds,
where the Goddess in you can finally rest,
but I am still here,
will still be here,
knocking on the door to love,
waiting for you to answer
and call me freak,
and call me Free,
and call me a bird that you blew out of its cage,
who just sits on your celestial finger
singing birdsongs to you in these love poems,
Dear One,
I am trying to come to terms
with losing you and it feels like
speaking without a tongue,
daytime without the sun,
please don't go, I love you.

I have become a woman in the embrace of your eyes,
blue skies that I have had the chance to hold…

Today, we demolished our shower together,
hammer and chisels breaking concrete and tile,
how you are always building, rebuilding, making new,
how you are perpetual creation,
and damn, I am lucky to have loved
and to love you each day,
how this conscious teaching and learning
has become something that brings us into an infinite loop,
a give and take,
a breath in and an exhale in gold,
my God,
I do love you,
I remember becoming a phoenix in your eyes,
and how much you put your fingers
in the fire,
telling me to burn.

⌘ Again, Again, Again

Maybe that was a vacuum, a crack in the ethers,
when you opened that door 8 years ago
and called me by my name,
took my light into your hands and shaped me into a god.

I feel like I've known you, dear,
like I knew you before all this unfolding of time and space,
before this infinite cosmic dance of light recognition.

I wear gold epaulettes on my shoulders
in place of the wings you know are there, and love,
don't stop reminding me that I flew here to meet you.

This is the beauty of our hearts converging.

I know your deja vu smile,
it tastes like every time the sun rises over the ocean,
I know infinity is a constant cycle
and I rejoice in finding you again, though I knew I would,
I knew that every footstep was a map etched in space,
every action created the equal and opposite reaction of your name
being written on my breastbone, love,
again, again, again, love.

I find you like the word "always,"
I find you like each time leaves come back to the empty limbs of trees,
I find you like saturn and her eternally circling rings,
I find you like every lost thing being found in the light of not ever being
    lost to you,
I find you like the unspooling of a quilt
    knit in the
        golden
            thread
                of consciousness
                    unravelling in all its subtle glory.

Maybe when you opened that door 8 years ago,
there was a ripple
in the ever-moving trajectory of infinity,
and the heart of the universe
skipped slightly in patterns of grace,
in patterns of our names
written side by side,
as they always have been,
as they always will be, love,

love, love, love,

again, again, again.

⌘ Mundan(c)e

Our lives have become
a common noiseless place,
we lay,
bodies like separate churches,
holding tight to the holy we use to call ours,
the communion of your soft white thighs,
lighted skin,
the slightest distance
between my warmth and your warmth
was too much,
the aching to be enraptured,
entwined,
where does this go?

Is my mouth still a prayer you send to the stars?
Can I bend
all of my limbs around you
and form anything but a home, love?
This ordinary quiet,
these separate worlds,
two bubbles repelling but
I need to find you,
I need to know again the shape of your kiss,
I miss the hours we spent becoming sunrise, love,
this mundane dance is not our story,
I will not walk by you without longing, wanting,
I cannot look at your face across our casual routine
without pining for those hours,
dying for the sounds our bodies made when becoming one song.

How does a love like ours become the hum of silent wanting,
this acceptance of not being viscerally in love,
this passionate disappearing, love?
I am aching to know again that I am your completion,
that I am the river and you are every ocean
waiting to be filled with
my rushing
toward
you.

⌘ Higher Eyes

You took me
outside
three times,
in a mixture of sleet and snow,
until the poet
in me
came out to play,
until intuition ruled over mind,
until my higher eyes opened
to the wonder of it all,
to notice the landscape
of a deadened winter
turn into the mystical slopes
and crunch of ice and white,
no need for a flashlight,
I followed the light of your starlit heart,
at the eleventh hour of night,
I could see it
ALL,
no moon,
billowing clouds,
north wind,
radiant snowfall,
and the entire landscape
glowing in an ice-laced winter gown,
every step leading to more beauty covering ground.

We found the hidden
streams that cut
through the wild
and joins our lake,
nature's arteries
that have been dry,
now rushing with the
promise of spring
disguised as one last lingering frost.

I kissed you while
you were expounding about
how the bridge we built
looks like a small town in Denmark,
and your lips
were soft and quiet,
the water sound rushing in whispers
that say
we are still
built more out of love
than anything else…

and you would bring me out
in a hurricane,
in a tornado,
in a tsunami
just to be swept up in
a moment of beauty
that the poet in me
needs to see.

⌘ Waiting For a Storm

It is windy inside the house,
and if I know anything, it's this,
you are always waiting for a storm,
you are kissing the breeze out loud
with the words of a story that
has been locked inside your chest for centuries,
opened treasure finding its way to now,
the bellows of our house singing a song of release
into the night air.

It is windy inside the house,
and I have always been one to hide from the rain,
you dance naked in it like a baptism,
like all of your sins
were borrowed so you could feel
the freedom in their washing away,
give them back to the earth,
for you are made of cosmos and diamonds,
you bend light into rainbows with your violet hands.

It is windy inside the house,
every moment is an adventure with you,
like nothing is impossible
and there is a mountain we have already climbed
if we just look down,
but the constellations above are too much like sisters
for us to care about what's under our feet,
let's keep dancing like this for hours,
in this symmetry of movement that we call our bodies.

It is windy inside the house,
we have turned out all the lights
and candles lantern our space in the wild,
the storm has passed with barely a drop,
but the lightning in my heart for you
is answered with the thunder of your voice
a second later, the storm is here.
The storm is us.

⌘ Fishing and Make Believe

She says
"let's build a fire
and roast weenies,"
it is Easter,
afternoon,
there is a slight mist,
she brings down a thick blanket, pillows,
(and if necessary)
a rain cover plastic sheet
built into a roof of bent sticks with
suspended cathedral ceiling,
and we make a house outside,
play family,
play make-believe
except this is real life,
and sometimes I can't believe
I am so lucky.

I build a circle out of
head-sized stones,
the jagged and smooth edges
form natural arcs,
give way to one another,
this stone to this stone to this stone,
I can feel the ritual shifting of rocks,
ancient lifetimes becoming visible,
unspoken masonry permeating silence,
the concentration of holding a fire
in a circle, unbroken,
housed.

The fire sizzles and smokes,
white fog billows from wet wood,
useless kindling I gathered
in the weather's indecision drizzle,
I hear her up by the house,

splitting dried logs,
the dogs listen, perked ears,
to the cock-a-doodle-doo
of the neighbors' rooster smoke alarm.

The sun pokes through clouds,
I sit on the edge of the deck
swinging my legs back and forth,
holding a bamboo stick,
imaginary fishing pole,
no line,
no hook,
no water,
but this may be the greatest catch of my life.

⌘ Meteor Shower / Meeting-Her Shower

This is the first time
we really made an effort
to watch the meteor showers
that are promised to be
quite a magnificent spectacle tonight.

Earlier she was running around the house,
going up and down to the garden
bringing supplies, a tiki torch,
the grass mat, pillows, sheets,
all the goods necessary for
a night time show in the expecting sky.

She made a bed for us outside on the deck
directly under a piece of open heavens carved out of treetops,
and we waited until the stars started peeking
out through the moonless twilight
before laying out on our spot of green.

The time had come.
Night had made enough of its mark over the face of day,
and we trudged down with champagne
to claim our meteor watching spot,
and I did not know I would be meeting her again.

We laid on our backs, balancing
champagne flutes on our laughing bellies,
delightful effervescence rising up to meet the stars,
jiggling giggled gold and glass,
our smiling mouths and bright eyes,
the open firmament,
and my love next to me, waiting for the gods
to connect the constellations with streaks of fire.

Silence echoed our loving whispers,
as we made out shapes and faces in the silhouettes of treetops,

and then WHOOOOOOOSH....
a slow fireball moves across our cutout plane of open sky,
flames trailing its fiery arc, and we *ooh* and *ahh*
and our pointing fingers meet in the air,
trace the fire-line flying then falling behind the mountain's horizon.

Look over there!
Ooh, another one there!
That one is huge!
Woooooooooooooooooow......

Fireball after fireball soars through
the dome of heavens,
and she points them out to me
like a mother showing her child every hidden wonder,
like a lover enchanting me with magic held in her hands,
this is no disappearing act,
this is forever and always, looking up together,
remember our starry homes,
knowing we will always meet where there is a trace of light.

Meteor shower,
this beautiful meeting-her shower
of love
between our wide open hearts,
under the stars,
I meet her again for the first time,
with all the wonder and magic and emotion
I have always held for her,
I lay back and tilt my head to face her,
I see the sky fire trails bouncing light off her blue eyes,
my personal domes of heaven I peer into
to find myself,
our entwined spirits take on fiery flight
and we ride through the atmosphere on the tails of meteors,
streaking our love story in light and fire

for all the world to see.

⌘ Hearing Underwater

I can hear myself better underwater,
when the soft horizon of wet
climbs the edges of bathtub white
and my skin dives below
the roaring whisper of rising water.

I lie down,
creating my own rolling wave,
as the force of my flesh pushes a small tsunami
backwards in a slow arch and forward
around my waist to the front opposite tub wall.
I can never get my entire body submerged,
hills of breast and belly
making whale dance ripples
of cold, the air still biting at what is
not underwater.

Head back, under,
my ears fill,
the nature of the body, plugging
the holes of sound until
I myself, become the stillness,
the slow breath of my bones
echoes like god noise,
like wind trapped in a bottle,
I listen.

I can hear myself better underwater,
become surround sound reverberation,
movement of slow floating,
I swim in the music a swallow makes,
a hum,
drinking myself in,
the resonance of my heartbeat like my chest has a new song.
It is a pulling to center,
when the waters envelope me,
a call back to the ocean where I am a
part of everything and everything is a part of me.
I say the beginnings of poem into the porcelain air,
and I can feel the earth hear.

⌘ Church Windows

Your tiny wings were like church windows,
golden stained glass
pouring wing-shaped light
over the stillness of the day,
catching sun
like a moving prism
that only reflects 24-karat wisdom,
soft, malleable, pure alchemical alloy
of dragonfly divinity.

I was floating on my back,
lounging deep into the heat of midday,
my feet, dainty, crossed over each other,
my toes freshly painted in summer fire,
my face kissing noon sun
wanting tan,
wanting a few shades darker,
almost brown body bobbing in backyard lake
made full with rain,
lake runneth over, spilling
into neighboring streams,
the only sound, the slow movement of water,
and I can never close my eyes,
never fully rest when I float from one shore to another,
still the ever-suspicious city girl in peaceful country home,
always suspect of snakes slithering
in the water to get me,
or some other uninvited scary nature thing
that's a threat to me,

but then you came…

golden dragonfly flight,
shaft of amber light buzzing
with the hum of divine,
swooping infinities around

my flame-painted orange toenails,
and I thought to myself smiling,
"maybe it will land on my toe"
and you hummed and hovered
like a tiny golden helicopter,
you flew toward my feet,
and I flinched!
almost toppling over into the water,
splash sending you ten feet high to
survey the fear of irrational humans.

I flinched!
How could I flinch at such beauty,
shy away from such golden perfection,
you landed on my red floaty beside my left leg
and I could almost hear your wise
and knowing golden laughter
break through the breezes and hot silence.

I acknowledged your presence and my silly fear.
I acknowledged the beauty and harmony of the moment,
and as soon as I accepted the gift
of your golden presence,
you flew upwards within seconds
and landed on my right big toe,
feet still crossed in a quiet prayer,
you landed as though I were a fragrant iris opening to morning,
you landed as though I were the tallest blade of lake grass
pointing upward to the sky,
you landed and became church and steeple
holding all this light in your wings and shining
it across the soft curve top of my foot,
painting me in golden gleam,
I dared not move, no,
just thanked you silently and watched you shift and turn,
prismatic dance of expanding and changing brilliance.

You see, maybe you are unaware of all the Light you hold,
the sun, in all its midday strength,

shoots beams into your open wings,
and maybe you can't see the glow in all your hum and buzz,
but the holy is there,
the golden stained glass that you become
is a breath that I forever hold in,
a gasp inward, as to draw in that same shine,
how your wings refract rays of sunlight for you to give away freely,
and you suddenly become the most luminary being,
and I suddenly become a girl, floating, who believes in angels.

⌘ ORION FRECKLES

I have freckles
on my right shoulder
that are the exact
pinpoint dot map of
the constellation
Orion,
like
the universe
can always
tap me there
to get my attention,
like,
"Hey look up!
Something beautiful's happening,"
like
my head sits
on the cusp of stars,
like
the time I broke my right collarbone
when I was 11,
and it never really healed
is probably so it could sit
in the perfect arch of *milky way,*
like
as above, so below,
like
this is a mirror to all the light I know,

and I remember
one new-moon night
when I looked out
over the glinting waters
of the caribbean sea,
I tilted my head up and,
found Orion on his side
and how, from here, he looks

like a butterfly
not so much a warrior,
and sometimes
I am a butterfly
not so much a warrior,

but did you know
the third brightest star
in Orion is *Bellatrix*,
a latin name meaning
"female warrior"
Orion's left shoulder,
opposite of Betelgeuse.
I found out about Bellatrix
while writing this poem,

but I think
she has always been
the darkest freckle
on my shoulder,
and when I look up
into the night's open mouth,
I think Bellatrix
is the brightest star
I've ever seen.

⌘ 11:11

Activate,
wake up the strands,
the dormant breath of a Soul
unawake but searching for purpose,
for light,
to be understood,
to recognize the stars in the eyes of my tribe,
activate,
awaken,
make a wish on my bones,
split my atoms
so that I am only light,
so that I speak in cosmic tongue
and my vibration is
in line with the vibration hum
of our moving, spinning, orbiting oneness,
our aligned ones,
ones aligned,
shoulder to shoulder,
welcoming a dawn of a new age,
a consciousness opening like a crystalline nebula
of prismatic triumph in space,
the stars are my brilliant regalia
for I know the constellation
that holds the flag for my sky,
I look up in the night and see a mirror
of my heavenly body,
my physical self
reflected in rays,
in ripples of love,
in waves of OMs that multiply in silent thoughts,
in constant repetition,
until everything around me
is circles, circles, circles,
loops, loops, loops,
spiral of this world,

"as above, so below,"
activate,
awaken,
breathe in the knowingness
of all of us waking up together,
this is history,
no mystery, we are here,
we are moving,
we are hurling towards the sun of a new beginning,
11:11,
master number,
binary code,
DNA alarm clock that activates the soul,
make me a beacon of your synchronicity,
I want my name to be light,
my movement to be flight,
my perils to be righted
in the name of transmutation,
lift my doldrums to the higher realms,
and turn them into the sound of bells ringing,
eternally,
bells ringing,
harbingers of spirits,
my heart is a cardinal song,
red in the morning sky,
11:11,
wake me up
and let me stay in this dream,
this freedom,
this sight,
this shift of thought into
knowing that I AM.

I AM.

I AM.

I AM.

⌘ THE CHAKRAS OF GOD / PLANETARY ALIGNMENT

If you look up
in the night sky tonight,
your naked eyes
will witness a spectacular
line up of spheres,
a conference of five planets
closest to earth,
convening in the dome of Heaven,
arcing above the horizon in a dance between stars.

Mercury kisses
the upper lip of our horizon
plays the quick sun chaser with its
predawn shine, the planet of the mind,
the illuminating principle of human life,
and no, not just the closest planet to the sun,
but emanating the energies of the higher realms,
the mercurial messenger of the Gods,
the closest planet to the SUN inside us,
facilitating the transmutation from personality to Soul,
this Mercury light,
bright in the sky's late night,
starts our necklace of otherworldly pearls.

Next in this celestial line up is Venus,
named for the Goddess of Love and Beauty,
the Feminine Divine in her glowing orbital triumph,
she shines brightest in the sky
and the ancients knew it was her eyes,
universal third eye of the night,
it was her breasts,
universal nourishment of mother, of woman,
it was her LOVE, it was her LOVE,
Venus, vehicle of the universal LOVE principle among men,
Venus, the spiritual mother of the ecliptic plane,
if a planet were home to me,

I feel it might be there,
the blue light that pulses inside me
moves to the rhythm of her swirling heat,
Venus,
the steady movement
of a mother's hip, mothership,
that I wish would call me back to her warmth,
her love melting the space between
her colder brothers.

Rings,
we can see Saturn's rings from
the telescope of our imaginations,
we all know they are there,
particles of ice and rock
hovering around the waist of a Golden Sphere,
Saturn is the Lord of Karma,
the Dweller on the Threshold,
the punisher and the payback,
the testing ground for the traveller on the Path,
if you have not seen the Gates of Initiation,
Saturn is just that planet with the rings,
but if you have jumped through his hoops
to reach the light of your own consciousness,
you know the weight of all of these things.

Mars is next
in this configuration in space,
red in all its glory,
scientists just found water on Mars,
but they have yet to see the blood of sacrifice on its spiritual surface,
the sacrifice of our Souls to the physical level of form,
the death of the soul to be born in the body,
the descent into matter,
to learn lessons in the World of Man,
the fall all the way down to earth, to rise,
this is Mars, the war of duality,
the fight between the Soul and the personality,
the red reflecting even on the darkest night,

the naked eye shroud of remembrance of what we have all done,
fallen from a place of light,
to bear the burden of knowing we must once again unite.

Hey, Jupiter,
nothing's been the same,
last in the line-up of giants
in our January canvas of night,
Jupiter is the far-off brightness of the other worlds,
the cusp of existences between the physical
and the eternal,
Jupiter,
great red spot heart swirling
a hurricane the size of three earths,
there is the red mixture of Love and Wisdom,
there is the energy of fusion
in which we as these mortal beings
can face the light of our ever-reaching Souls,
Jupiter is the ruler of blessings for Humanity,
the manifestation of us all holding hands,
of right human relations through the vehicle of Love and Wisdom,
it is triumph over the lower worlds we harbor within
to the victory of oneness and collective consciousness.

This is not the science of the mundane,
but the fact of the Supermundane that pulses with life
in the fibers of every atom and every infinitely splitting cell,
this is the one life that speaks in the mouths of rivers,
that breathes in the wind through trees,
that undulates in waves that end on the shore of Self,
this is how we recognize each other
when we are looking with the eyes of our Souls.

Look up in the sky,
the Heavens are offering you a window
to the Higher Worlds,
the chakras of the Universe are displayed in naked eye wonder,
laying across the hemisphere like a constellation called God,
these planets are not others, but part of the whole,

as much as we are part of the whole,
the energies of these five giants are pouring into us
and we are a little blue dot with open arms,
needing all the help we can get.

Look in the sky tonight,
open your arms and face to the bright lights
that are trying to make it all the way down to you,
so your heart

can feel

EVERY HEART.

⌘ Petals

How do you craft the light
of a lotus petal on fire in space?
How can you measure that much brightness,
with earthly eyes and human fingers?

What does a group of Souls, alive and soaring,
reflect in the Heavenly Spheres?

A rainbow?
A nebula?
A supernova, glimmering and
glinting in the inhalations and exhalations
of the Source of ALL things?

There are stars in your hand.
There are stars in mine.
Let's point them to the edge of infinity and leave them there,
strewn into a constellation of hope rising
on the horizon of humanity's awakening.

This moment is a wakened dream
where there are no more questions like,
"Can I?"
"Will I?"
"Am I?"

There is no more circling endless doubt and muffled fear,

only, "Yes, I can. Yes, I will."
and
    "I AM HERE."

⌘ Launch

I am balancing
on a spinning planet,
holding myself down
to the ground with my toes clenched,
ready to spring into the abyss of space,
the wonderful blackness pinpricked with stars,
ready to rejoin everything that I see as light
from down here.

⌘ The Journey to the Self
(for my Teacher, Joann Saraydarian)

"The legendary forbidden fruit is the Self."—David McFadden

"Are you living like an ant, when your destination is the stars?"—Torkom Saraydarian

There is the
self,
look in the mirror,
in all of your
unmade-up glory,
in the pureness of fresh face
and solitude,
witness that self,
without judgement,
the self
with the lowercase s, self
small you,
small you that
does not dream outside boxes,
or color outside lines,
small you that is driven by
the ego,
glamour and illusion,
the perpetuation of your own small self,
the subconsciously-sleeping self
that only cares about personal gain,
the narrow view of *me*,
the importance placed on money,
on standards of richness based on
a succession of numbers that
never add up to *value*,
see the machine,
the movements,
the dance you perform to live,
to think you're living,

to think that this is what living is all about,
until you meet
someone
who has found
the Self.

the Self,
with the capital S, Self,
the S that stands up taller because
it is striving to reach
the eternal,
to taste the blaze inside,
the Self that has become
the infinite atom ever expanding into space,
unfolding into Lotus Jewels,
a spark of fire becoming One with the Sun
the light,
    the Light,
        the LIGHT

that each little self has the potential to Become.

I was going through the motions,
moving about as a numbed
unwinged thing,
imprisoned in a state
of inertia,
a bird in a cage
who only knew how to walk,
never to fly,
the iron bars of situations
forming a circle of illusion around me,
and there I lived,
without living,
there I dreamed of a song
I never knew how to sing,
there I wished for something greater
that I did not have the words to define,
a bird walking back and forth in that grey cage,

until one day, a door opened
physically and on all of the other levels concurrently,
and I met a Teacher of Souls,
a woman who
immediately knew my
Greater Destiny,
a woman who could see
my Light, though I had learned to hide it,
a woman who could recognize
the highest in me,
who tapped into the ocean
of my subconscious
and gave me a glimpse
of who I could be,
if I took the time
to remove the chains
of what I thought controlled me,
if I did the work
it took to face every demon
that I became,
if I carefully ripped off the armor
of emotional paralysis
and really looked all of the pain
square in the eyes,
if I went back to the beginning
and called each disaster by name,
if I realized that the key
to my own freedom
was shaped like my heart
and the only one that could open
the cage was my self, that self
striving to become my Self.

I did the work,
I fought every dark hole
that I fell into with my bare fists,
until I realized that I was punching myself,
every subconscious image I had built of me,
every false mask that I had learned to wear,

those shells showed themselves
and I did not recognize them as
me anymore, did not feel the security
of hiding inside them, because
when you put a false shell in a fire, it burns like hell,
when you stand eye to eye with
a Teacher holding a mirror,
you stop flinching at the shadows
you stop flailing fists of anger,
and learn to destroy the masks
with understanding and detachment,
you start to look at your life from a higher perspective,
you look at experiences from everyone's different points of view,
you see life from the eyes of a star instead of a stone.
This is half of the work,
this dark night of the soul,
this dweller on the threshold of becoming,
I lingered there for years,
illusions held my ankles
and dragged me underwater many times,
under the level of consciousness
I was trying to attain and back into the abyss
of subconscious drives, of dark thoughts,
of jealousy and blame,
glamour and ego,
the behaviors that were not
my True Self,
everyone's dark night of the soul has its own time table,
there are karmic lessons that sometimes
have to be learned over
and over
and over,
until that last shell that you are
desperately clinging to falls away
and you are a newborn
winged thing,
a fledgling soul on the precipice of flight,
and you know,
for the first time

that the winds of your own Light
will carry you to the dawn
of Greater Understanding and Love,
of Oneness and Beauty.

This is the journey to the Self,
the journey you do not know you are on
until you start to come out of the fog
you call home, the sleep
that you call life,
the numb that you call feeling,
this is the journey to the Self,
"Know Thyself!"
the forbidden fruit of Self-actualization
is not really forbidden,
but you are made to believe that it is,
you are trained by your own set of ideologies
that there should be no ever-reaching out,
and that comfortable hovel is a cheery
afternoon dwelling for your inert consciousness,
but it is NOT!

There is an expanse of stars
that know you by name,
cosmos inside your chest that hums
a harmony you have always known,
suns that look back when you stare
into that mirror,
LOOK AGAIN, BRIGHT ONE.
Look again, and see
that the steps in front of you
are steps that you are destined to climb,
that there is a mountain
inside your heart
and you *are* that mountain,
and you *are* that wind,
and you *are* the flag flying at the summit
and that flag sings of *your* name,
the Self, the Soul,
the Being of Light and Love Eternal.

Your sealed fate,
the fate of all human beings
is to transcend being human,
is to transcend these bodies
that surround us in fleshy limitation,
and realize that we can FLY,
that birds are not meant to walk
and the iron bars are invisible illusions
designed to keep us confined,
but there is no stopping
the evolution of the human consciousness,
there is no stopping
the colossal WAKING that is taking place
in every corner of this cornerless sphere we call earth,
we are waking up boundless,
we are taking our liberties back on a global scale,
we are looking darkness and corruption and evil in the eyes
and standing like a wall against it all,
a wall of unity in consciousness,
a wall of LOVE built with bricks of LIGHT,
impenetrable, unbreakable, destiny,
our VOICES joining together
to create a frequency that will shatter
anything that defies the greater good of mankind,
WE are standing,
because inside, YOU are starting to stand,
YOU are realizing that there is more
to existence that just existing,
when you know you can dream in color,
when you know that there is no time and space
and that everything is a
SYMPHONY OF ONE.

This is the journey to the Self,
this is being soul-infused,
seeing one as everything,
seeing the big picture in the little frame,
and calling it by name,
it is difficult to contain in words,
there are too many words to describe the sensation,

yet, silence would be more accurate,
beautiful and simple silence,
words tie strings
to the stringless kite of the Soul,
let it fly,
let it be,
know that you are that kite,
you are that diamond,
rising in these S formations,
being carried on the wind to achieve
the absolute humming stillness of actualization,
the eternal fire of joining
with who you always were,
who you always are,
who you forever will be,

LIGHT

    UNFOLDING

        INFINITELY.

About the Author

Kai Coggin is a poet and author living on the side of a small mountain in Hot Springs National Park, AR. She holds a BA in Poetry and Creative Writing from Texas A & M University. Kai writes poems on love, spiritual striving, injustice, metaphysics, and beauty. Her work has been published or is forthcoming in *Blue Heron Review*, *Lavender Review*, *Broad!*, *The Tattooed Buddha*, *Split This Rock*, *Yellow Chair Review*, *Drunk Monkeys*, *Harbinger Asylum*, *Snapdragon*, *ANIMA*, *Elephant Journal*, and many other literary journals, as well as anthologized in several international collections.

Kai is the author of a chapbook, *In Other Words* (2013), and two full-length collections, *PERISCOPE HEART* (Swimming with Elephants Publications, 2014) and *WINGSPAN* (Golden Dragonfly Press, 2016). Her poetry has recently been nominated for The Pushcart Prize and Bettering American Poetry 2015. She is the curator of Words & Wine, an adult creative writing class at Emergent Arts in Hot Springs. She is also a Teaching Artist with the Arkansas Arts Council, specializing in bringing poetry and creative writing to youth across the state.

If you would like to contact Kai to arrange a poetry reading, a classroom visit, a speaking engagement, or a book signing in your area, please e-mail her at kaicoggin@gmail.com.

www.kaicoggin.com

Made in the USA
Charleston, SC
26 May 2016